SCHOLASTIC

Easy
**Make & Learn
Projects**

Weather

by Donald M. Silver and Patricia J. Wynne

NEW YORK • TORONTO • LONDON • AUCKLAND • SYDNEY
MEXICO CITY • NEW DELHI • HONG KONG • BUENOS AIRES

Teaching
Resources

For Mike Gordon,

Silent Strength,

Loving Heart

—D M S

To Breezy,

The pilot who taught me

to love the weather

—P J W

Editor: Maria L. Chang
Cover and interior design by Kathy Massaro

ISBN: 978-0-439-45336-3
Copyright © 2011 by Donald M. Silver and Patricia J. Wynne
All rights reserved.
Printed in the U.S.A.

2 3 4 5 6 7 8 9 10   40   20 19 18 17 16 15 14 13 12 11

Contents

Introduction

Students are probably more familiar with the weather and how it works than they suspect. Depending on the weather, they determine what kinds of clothes to wear and whether they can go outside to play. They often hear adults discussing the weather. When the television or radio is on, they may pick up bits and pieces of a local weather report. And when disaster strikes in the form of a powerful hurricane or tornado, they quickly understand how serious the impact of weather can be on the lives of families and communities.

Children know that puddles disappear long before they understand what evaporation is. They respond to the roar of thunder or flashes of lightning without understanding how one causes the other. When the sky darkens, they are pretty sure it will rain. When heavy snow falls, they secretly hope school will be canceled. Depending on where they live, children can pretty much predict what the weather will be like as the seasons change.

The 15 easy-to-make and easy-to-read mini-books and manipulatives in this book are designed to expand upon and extend students' knowledge of the weather and how it works. The mini-books and manipulatives meet the earth science curriculum standards, teaching concepts such as:

❋ Weather changes from day to day and over the seasons.

❋ Weather can be described by measurable quantities, such as temperature, wind direction and speed, and precipitation.

❋ Water in the air exists in different forms (e.g., clouds, water vapor) and changes from one form to another through various processes (e.g., evaporation, condensation, precipitation).

❋ The sun provides the light and heat necessary to maintain the Earth's temperature.

❋ Air is a substance that surrounds us, takes up space, and moves around us as wind.

Students will also learn how to identify clouds, how storms form, how weather is measured, how to read a weather map, what climate is, and how global warming affects us.

What's Inside

The mini-books and manipulatives are independent and can be used in any order. Within each chapter are lessons that feature the following:

❋ **Weather Center:** Background information for teaching the lesson

❋ **Making the Mini-book or Manipulative:** Easy-to-follow instructions with diagrams for assembling the mini-book or manipulative

- **Teaching With the Mini-book or Manipulative:** Discussion questions for after reading

- **More to Do:** Further activities to extend learning

- **Resources:** Related books and Web sites

- **Reproducible Pages:** Templates for each mini-book or manipulative to be distributed to students

Helpful Hints

As with any new instructional material, it is always a good idea to make the mini-books and manipulatives yourself before introducing them to your class. This way, you can anticipate any questions that may arise and be ready to help students as needed. When students are ready to assemble their own mini-books and manipulatives, you may want to model the steps for them and invite them to follow along. Or, present your finished mini-book or manipulative as a guide they can study as they make their own.

Keep in mind:

- The thickest solid lines on the reproducible pages are CUT lines. Dashed lines are FOLD lines.

- Some mini-books and manipulatives have interior flaps that require cutting. An easy way to cut them is to use the "pinch method": Use your thumb and forefinger to fold the paper near one line and, taking your scissors, snip an opening. Then insert the scissors through the opening to easily cut out the flaps.

- If possible, enlarge the pattern pages to make the mini-books and manipulatives easier for students to assemble.

- If students plan to color the mini-books and manipulatives and use tape, have them color first so they won't have to color over the tape.

- Encourage students to bring their mini-books and manipulatives home and share them with their families. You may also want to put additional copies and extra materials in a learning center so that students can make and read them on their own.

We hope that you and your students get as much fun and excitement out of these mini-books and manipulatives as we had in creating them. Enjoy!

Where Weather Takes Place

**Learn about the layers of the atmosphere—
including the layer in which weather takes place—
with this mobile.**

Weather Center

Weather is the condition of the atmosphere at any given time or place. The *atmosphere* is an ocean of air that surrounds the Earth and extends from the surface out into space. Air is a mixture of colorless, odorless gas molecules. Nitrogen makes up about 78 percent of air, oxygen about 21 percent, and carbon dioxide and water vapor gas make up less than 1 percent. Trace amounts of other gases, such as argon, neon, helium, xenon, krypton, and hydrogen, as well as dust and dirt particles, make up the rest of air.

Most of these gas molecules can be found in the lowest layer of the atmosphere. The atmosphere has four layers. The lowest layer, or the *troposphere*, touches the Earth's surface and extends up between 5 and 10 miles (8 to 16 km). The air in the troposphere is warmest near the Earth's surface. The higher up it goes, the colder the air gets. Nearly all weather takes place in the troposphere. Above the troposphere is the *stratosphere*, which continues up to about 30 miles (50 km) above the Earth's surface. Not much weather takes place in this layer. However, ozone gas in the upper stratosphere soaks up the sun's harmful ultraviolet rays, which can cause skin cancers in people. Extending up to about 50 miles (80 km) is the third layer, or *mesosphere*. Gas molecules in this layer are spread out very far apart. The fourth layer, or *thermosphere*, reaches hundreds of miles into space. There are almost no gases in the thermosphere, and no weather takes place in it or in the mesosphere.

Materials

* Reproducible pages 8–10
* Scissors
* Tape
* Hole puncher
* Crayons, colored pencils, or markers (optional)

Making the Mini-book

1 Photocopy pages 8–10. Color, if desired.

2 Cut out all the pieces along the thick, solid, outer lines. Set aside the circle on page 10.

3 Cut open the four solid, semicircular lines on page 1 of the mini-book, making sure to stop where the solid lines end.

4 Fold pages 1 and 2 of the book back-to-back along the center dashed line so the text is facing out. Repeat for pages 3 and 4.

5 Use a hole puncher to open the four small circles on the mobile hanging pieces on page 10. Fold the two mobile hanging pieces along the dashed lines. Insert one of the pieces between pages 1 and 2, as shown, and tape it in place. Insert the other in exactly the same position between pages 3 and 4 and tape. Tape closed the open sides of the pages.

6 Tape pages 1–2 together to 3–4 along the left spine to create the mini-book. The holes on the mobile hanging pieces should be directly on top of each other.

7 Take the circle you had set aside and cut open the inner semicircular, solid lines, making sure to stop where the solid lines end.

8 Turn to page 4 of the mini-book. Place the left side of the circle piece on the spot that says TAPE FOUR-LAYER PIECE HERE, as shown. Be sure the words on the circle are right side up and readable. Tape the piece in place so it extends over the right side of the book.

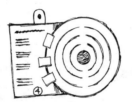

9 Turn the mini-book over to page 1 and fold and lift the two halves of the cut-open piece, as shown. Encourage students to hang their book mobiles, using the holes at the top of the mini-book.

Teaching With the Mini-book

Invite students to color, assemble, and read their mini-books. Then check for understanding by asking them these questions:

1 What is the atmosphere? *(The ocean of air that flows around the Earth)*

2 What is weather? *(The state of the atmosphere at any given time)*

3 What is air made of? *(Gases like nitrogen, oxygen, and carbon dioxide)*

4 What are the four layers of the atmosphere? *(Troposphere, stratosphere, mesosphere, and thermosphere)*

5 Where does most weather take place? *(In the lowest layer, or troposphere)*

More to Do

Weather Words

Work with students to generate a list of the different states of the atmosphere, or weather. The list could include words such as *hot*, *warm*, *cool*, *cold*, *windy*, *clear*, *cloudy*, *rainy*, *sunny*, *snowy*, and so on. Once a day for a week, have students look out the windows and describe the weather outside using the list of words.

Resources

What's the Weather
(Scholastic, 2008)

By lifting flaps and turning wheels, children discover what weather is and what makes it change. Also includes a fun weather game.

http://earthguide.ucsd.edu/earthguide/diagrams/atmosphere/index.html

Click the buttons on this site to find out about height, temperature, layer names, and other information about the Earth's atmosphere.

Where Does Weather Happen?

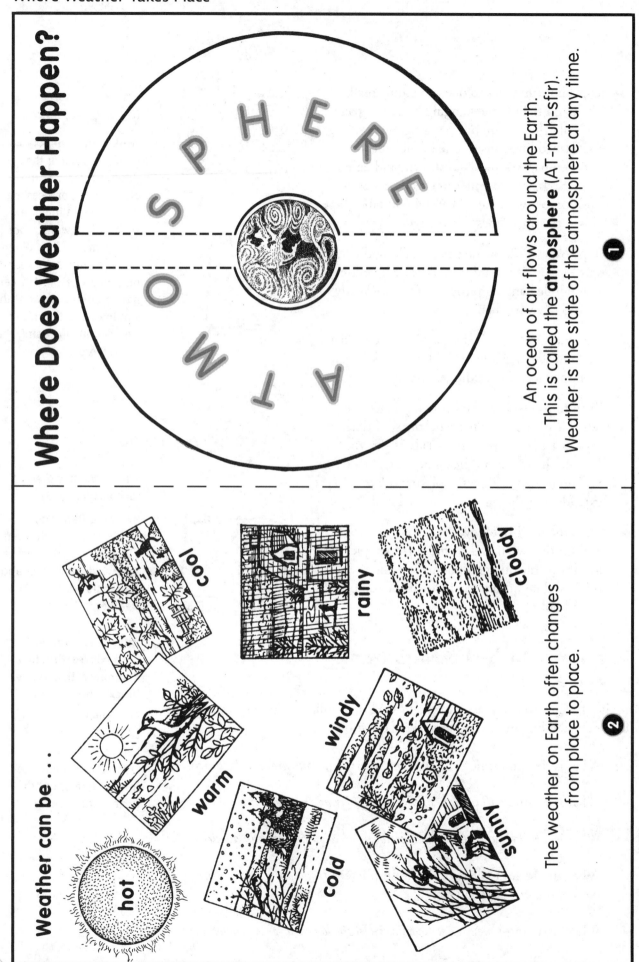

S P H E R E
A T M O

An ocean of air flows around the Earth.
This is called the **atmosphere** (AT-muh-sfir).
Weather is the state of the atmosphere at any time.

❶

Weather can be . . .

cool

rainy

cloudy

warm

windy

cold

sunny

hot

The weather on Earth often changes
from place to place.

❷

Easy Make & Learn Projects: Weather © 2011 by Donald M. Silver and Patricia J. Wynne, Scholastic Teaching Resources

❸

Air is made up of gases like nitrogen, oxygen, and carbon dioxide.

You can't see them or smell them.

Plants take in carbon dioxide from the air to make food.

We breathe in air to get oxygen to stay alive.

There is also water in the air.

Most of the water in air is in the form of gas (water vapor). Some of it is in tiny droplets that make up clouds.

Tape four-layer piece here.

❹

The atmosphere has four layers.

We live in the lowest layer, the **troposphere** (TROH-puh-sfir). Nearly all weather happens here.

Above the troposphere is the **stratosphere** (STRA-tuh-sfir). It contains ozone gas that soaks up harmful rays from the sun.

The **mesosphere** (MEH-zuh-sfir) is the third layer. The gases here are very far apart.

The fourth layer, or **thermosphere** (THUHR-muh-sfir), reaches into space. It has very little gas.

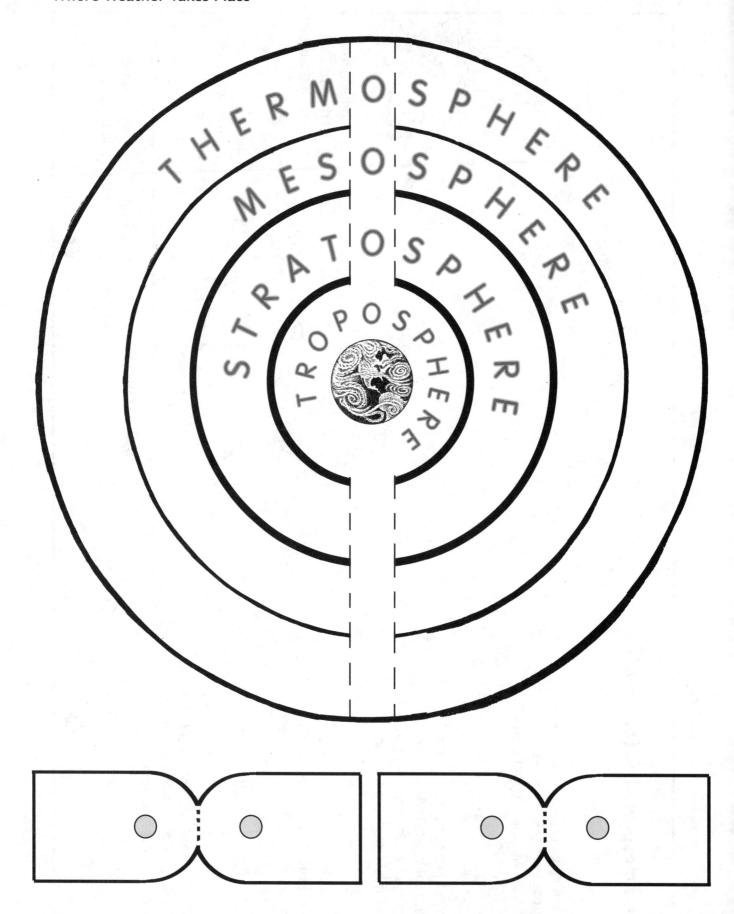

Easy Make & Learn Projects: Weather © 2011 by Donald M. Silver and Patricia J. Wynne, Scholastic Teaching Resources

The Sun and the Weather

Linked sun and Earth mini-books explain how the sun's energy affects weather on Earth.

Weather Center

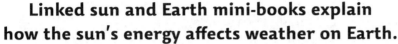

The sun is the only star in our solar system. It is a gigantic ball of extremely hot gases—one million Earths could fit inside the sun! The sun's center generates vast amounts of energy that rise to the surface and radiate into space. After traveling about 93 million miles (150 million km) through space, the sun's energy—in the form of light and heat—reaches the Earth, supporting life on our planet. Because the sun radiates energy in all directions into space, the Earth receives less than one-billionth of the energy the sun gives off.

Some of this energy that reaches the Earth bounces back into space. Clouds and gases in the atmosphere soak up some energy, warming up the air a little (see page 76). Heat energy that reaches the Earth's surface, however, is soaked up by soil, rocks, water, animals, plants, people, buildings, and so on, warming them all up. Heat then rises from the warmed land and water and, in turn, warms the air above them. The gas molecules in the warm air move faster and spread out. As its molecules spread out, the warm air becomes lighter and rises. It carries heat upward, gives off heat, and raises the surrounding air temperature. When air gives off heat, its gas molecules slow down and move closer together. The air then cools, becomes heavier, and sinks. The sinking cool air flows under the rising warm air and replaces it. Heat from the land or water warms the sinking cool air and the process repeats.

This repeating process, which starts from the sun, drives weather on Earth. The air does not warm up all at once. It takes time for the process to repeat over and over and for the air temperature to rise. That's why the warmest part of the day isn't noon but rather mid-afternoon. At night, when the sun's energy can't reach part of the Earth, the land and water cool down, as does the air. The temperature then drops until a new day begins.

Making the Mini-book

1 Photocopy pages 13–15. Color, if desired.

2 Cut out all the pieces along the thick, solid lines.

Materials

❋ Reproducible pages 13–15

❋ Scissors

❋ Tape

❋ Crayons, colored pencils, or markers (optional)

More to Do

Earth's Heater

On a sunny day, take the class outdoors early in the morning. Invite children to feel the soil, rocks, concrete in the schoolyard, and the wall of the school itself. Do they feel warm or cool? You may even have them record the temperature outside. Repeat the activity later in the afternoon. Ask: Do the objects feel warmer in the morning or in the afternoon? After rereading their books, challenge students to explain what is warming the objects and how those warmed objects affect the air that touches them.

Resources

The Sun
by Melanie Chrismer
(Children's Press, 2008)

Students learn about the sun—what it is, how hot and bright it gets, and how it gives off light and heat.

http://www.nasa.gov/vision/universe/solarsystem/sun_for_kids_main.html

NASA's Web site explains why scientists study the sun and lists the top 10 sun facts everyone should know. Don't miss the "Sun For Kids" video and other amazing videos.

3 Fold pages 1 and 2 of "The Sun and the Weather" mini-book back-to-back along the dashed line so the text is facing out. Tape the pages together, as shown.

4 Place pages 1–2 on top of page 3, so the arrow faces the right side of the book. Tape the mini-book pages together along the left spine.

5 Fold pages 4 and 5 of the "Earth" mini-book back-to-back along the dashed line so the text is facing out. Tape the pages together. Repeat with pages 6 and 7.

6 Place pages 4–5 on top of pages 6–7. Tape the pages together along the left spine, as shown.

7 Tape the head of the arrow on top of the "Earth" mini-book, as shown.

Teaching With the Mini-book

Invite students to color, assemble, and read their mini-books. Then check for understanding by asking them these questions:

1 What makes the weather on Earth keep changing? *(Energy from the sun)*

2 What is the sun? *(A huge star made up of very hot gases; it creates vast amounts of energy that comes in different forms, such as heat and light.)*

3 What warms up the land? *(Energy from the sun)*

4 What happens to air when it touches the warmed land? *(It warms up and rises; cooler air takes its place.)*

5 What happens at night? *(There is no direct energy from the sun so the land cools down. The air cools down, and the temperature drops.)*

The Sun and the Weather

What makes the weather on Earth change all the time? Energy from the sun!

1

The sun is a star made up of very hot gases. About one million Earths could fit inside the huge sun!

2

Easy Make & Learn Projects: Weather © 2011 by Donald M. Silver and Patricia J. Wynne, Scholastic Teaching Resources

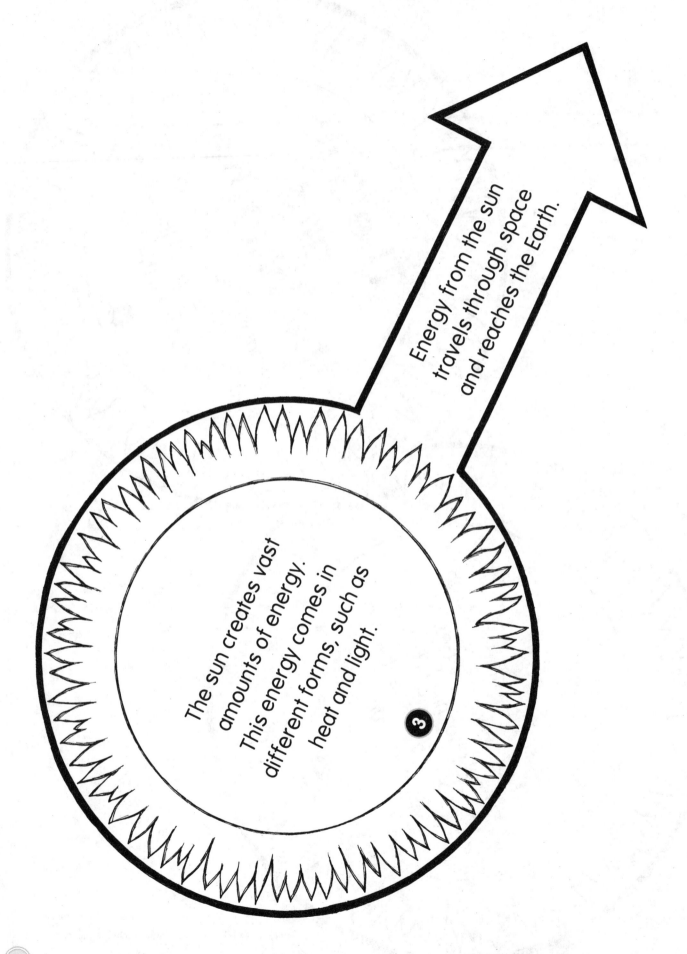

Energy from the sun travels through space and reaches the Earth.

The sun creates vast amounts of energy. This energy comes in different forms, such as heat and light.

3

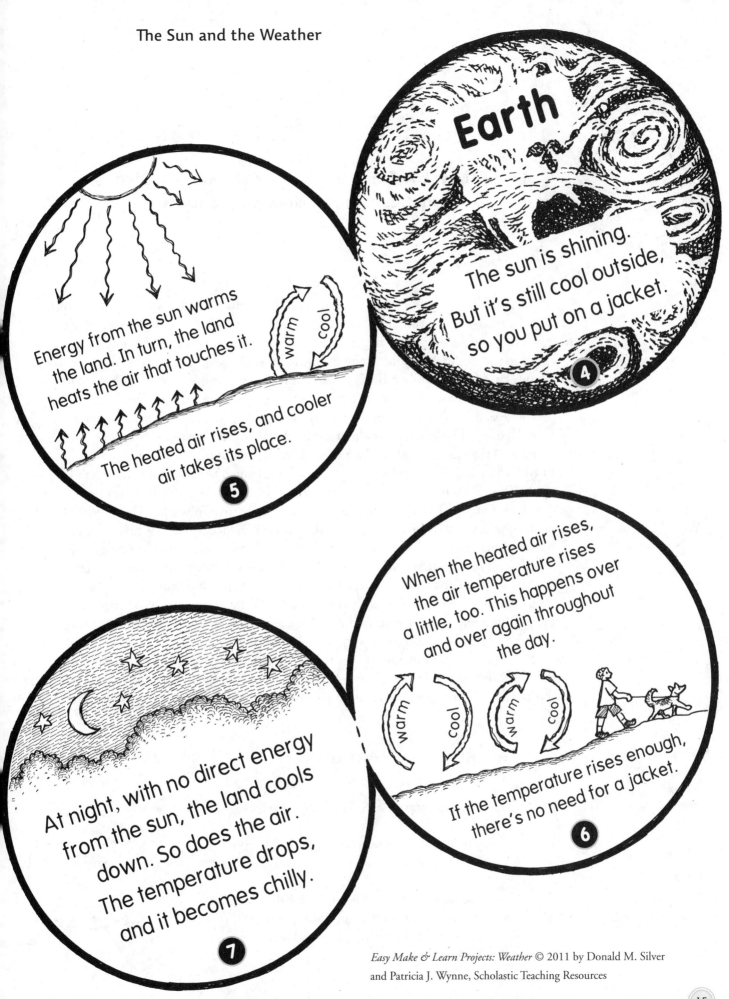

Earth

The sun is shining.
But it's still cool outside,
so you put on a jacket.

4

Energy from the sun warms the land. In turn, the land heats the air that touches it.

warm cool

The heated air rises, and cooler air takes its place.

5

When the heated air rises, the air temperature rises a little, too. This happens over and over again throughout the day.

warm cool warm cool

If the temperature rises enough, there's no need for a jacket.

6

At night, with no direct energy from the sun, the land cools down. So does the air. The temperature drops, and it becomes chilly.

7

Easy Make & Learn Projects: Weather © 2011 by Donald M. Silver and Patricia J. Wynne, Scholastic Teaching Resources

The Seasons

Follow the Earth as it orbits the sun to learn what causes the changing seasons.

Weather Center

The Earth orbits around the sun. It takes the Earth 365.25 days—one year—to complete one orbit, or *revolution*. The path Earth follows is close to an ellipse, not a circle. So in January, the Earth is nearly 3 million miles (5 million km) closer to the sun than in July. Many people mistakenly believe that this is why seasons change. But while this might explain why it is summer in the southern half of the Earth in January, it doesn't explain why it is winter in the northern half.

The reason for seasons is because Earth's axis is tilted and its surface is curved. Earth's axis is an imaginary line that runs from the North Pole to the South Pole. The axis is tilted at an angle of 23.5 degrees from straight up and down. As the tilted Earth revolves around the sun, the seasons change. When the northern half of the Earth is tilted toward the sun, the Northern Hemisphere experiences summer as the sun's rays strike this part of Earth more directly than in winter. The Southern Hemisphere, which is tilted away from the sun, experiences winter. When the Earth moves to the other side of the sun, the Northern Hemisphere is tilted away from the sun. The sun's rays are spread out over a greater area of land on the Earth's curved surface, reducing the amount of solar energy the land and water can absorb. As a result, the air is colder in winter than in summer. At the same time, the Southern Hemisphere, which is tilted toward the sun, experiences summer. In winter, days are shorter and nights are longer; in summer, the reverse is true.

At the start of autumn and spring, the Earth is neither tilted toward or away from the sun. There are 12 hours of daylight and 12 hours of night. When it is spring in the Northern Hemisphere, it is autumn in the Southern Hemisphere, and vice versa.

Materials

* Reproducible pages 18–20
* Scissors
* Tape
* Brad (paper fastener)
* Crayons, colored pencils, or markers (optional)

Making the Manipulative

1 Photocopy pages 18–20. Color, if desired.

2 Cut out all the pieces along the thick, solid outer lines.

3 Position the black dot on the Earth piece under the black dot on the sun. Push the brad through the sun and the other piece and secure at the back.

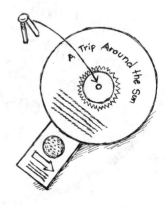

4 On the pieces that show the Earth at different times of the year, fold down the flaps along the dashed lines, as shown.

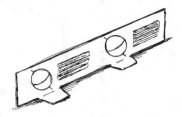

5 Tape the two pieces together on both ends so that they form a circle with the text on the inside.

6 Position the circular piece on the sun piece so that the flap with the black dot is on top of the matching shape with the black dot. Tape the flap in place. Tape the other flaps in place.

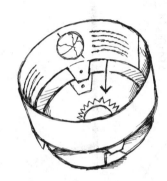

7 Tape the WINTER piece on the outside of the circle across from "December 21," as shown. To its right, tape SPRING (across from "March 20"), then SUMMER (across from "June 21"), then finally AUTUMN (across from "September 21").

Teaching With the Manipulative

Invite students to color, assemble, and read their manipulatives. To use, have students move the Earth around the sun, starting at June 21, and read about the Earth's position and its corresponding season. Then check for understanding by asking them these questions:

1 How long does it take Earth to make one complete trip around the sun? *(One year)*

2 What causes the seasons to change? *(The tilt of the Earth's axis)*

3 On December 21, when the northern half of the Earth is tilted away from the sun, what season is it there? *(Winter)*

4 Compare summer and winter weather. *(Summer days are long and hot, while nights are short and warm. In the winter, days are shorter and colder, and nights are longer and colder. The sun rises high in the sky in summer, but sits low in the sky in the winter.)*

5 At the start of which seasons is the Earth not tilted toward or away from the sun? *(Autumn and spring)*

More to Do

Tilted

Use a tilted globe and a flashlight to show how the sun's rays fall on the Earth's surface as the seasons change. Explain the relationship between the tilt of the Earth and where the most direct rays of sunlight strike over the course of a year. Students can easily see that when the Northern Hemisphere is tilted toward the sun, the light from the flashlight strikes that area more directly that when it is tilted away from the sun.

Resources

***The Reason for Seasons* by Gail Gibbons (Holiday House, 1996)**

Using simple words and colorful illustrations, this classic book explain what makes the seasons change in the Northern and Southern hemispheres.

http://www.astronomy. org/programs/seasons

Created by the Allentown School District Planetarium, this Web site features detailed pictures that explain why seasons change.

September 21

The Earth is not tilted toward the sun or away from it. Both north and south get the same amount of sunlight. Autumn begins in the north, while spring begins in the south.

June 21

The northern half of the Earth is tilted toward the sun. The southern half is tilted away. So the northern half gets more sunlight than the southern half. Summer begins in the north, while winter begins in the south.

December 21

The northern half of the Earth is tilted away from the sun. It gets less sunlight than the southern half. Winter begins in the north, and summer begins in the south.

March 20

The Earth is not tilted toward the sun or away from it. What season begins in the northern half of the Earth? What about in the south?

Easy Make & Learn Projects: Weather © 2011 by Donald M. Silver and Patricia J. Wynne, Scholastic Teaching Resources

A Trip Around the Sun

Sun

The Earth orbits around the sun. It takes the Earth one year to travel all the way around. As it travels around the sun, the Earth also rotates on its own axis. The Earth's axis is tilted. Sometimes the Earth is tilted toward the sun. Sometimes it's tilted away. This causes the seasons to change.
Move the Earth around the sun to learn more.

The Seasons

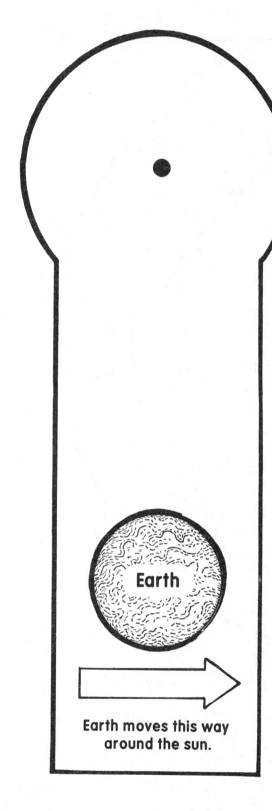

Earth

Earth moves this way
around the sun.

Spring

In spring, days start getting
longer. It's warmer than in
winter, but not as hot as in
summer. It often rains.

Summer

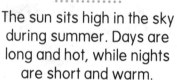

The sun sits high in the sky
during summer. Days are
long and hot, while nights
are short and warm.

Autumn

The nights start getting
longer in autumn.
The temperature gets
cooler. Many plants lose
their leaves.

Winter

It's winter. The sun sits
low in the sky. The days
are short, and nights
are long. In cold places,
snow falls.

Easy Make & Learn Projects: Weather © 2011 by Donald M. Silver and Patricia J. Wynne, Scholastic Teaching Resources

Clouds

**Identify different kinds of clouds and the types
of weather they bring with this mini-book.**

Weather Center

Clouds are made up of billions of tiny water droplets or ice crystals that float in the air. Air almost always has water in it. This water is in the form of a gas called *water vapor*. When the air temperature cools enough, some water vapor *condenses*—changes from gas to tiny liquid water droplets that form clouds. If the air keeps cooling, the droplets can join together, enlarge, and eventually fall as *precipitation* (see page 26) from the clouds.

Clouds come in different sizes and shapes. High clouds form above 18,000 feet (5,500 m), while low clouds form below 6,500 feet (1,980 m). In between, middle clouds are found. There are three main kinds of clouds—*cirrus, cumulus,* and *stratus*. High, feathery cirrus clouds can mean the weather is going to change. Because these clouds form so high in the sky, the water droplets in cirrus and cirrostratus clouds are frozen as ice crystals. When sunlight or moonlight passes through the ice crystals, the light rays bend and produce a ring around the sun or moon. Thick, puffy cumulus clouds usually signal fair weather. Gray layers of stratus clouds form low in the sky and often block out the sun and bring drizzles. When clouds block the sun during the day, they help cool the air. At night, clouds help keep heat rising from the Earth from escaping into space.

There are different kinds of storm clouds. Thick layers of dark nimbostratus clouds usually bring rain or snow. Cumulonimbus, or thunderclouds, are discussed in detail on page 41. Point out to students that on a foggy day they are actually walking through clouds, since fog is a cloud that touches the ground.

Making the Mini-book

1 Photocopy pages 23–25. Color, if desired.

2 Cut out all the pieces along the thick, solid, outer lines.

3 Fold cloud pieces 1, 2, and 3 along the dashed lines. Tape the folded flap of each cloud piece to its respective spot under the title CLOUDS. The clouds will pop up on the page.

Materials

* Reproducible pages 23–25

* Scissors

* Tape

* Crayons, colored pencils, or markers (optional)

More to Do

What's in a Name?

While there are three main cloud types—cirrus, cumulus, stratus—there are other clouds, such as cirrostratus, that are combinations of these main types. Still other clouds, such as altostratus, have prefixes that help describe them. The prefix *alto-* means "high." Have students research and describe different kinds of clouds, such as stratocumulus, cirrocumulus, altocumulus, and all of the clouds in their mini-books. Their descriptions should include cloud shape, color, altitude, weather predictions, and so on.

Resources

The Kids' Book of Clouds & Sky by Frank Staub (Sterling, 2005)

This question-and-answer book about clouds comes with excellent photos that kids are sure to find appealing.

http://www. weatherwizkids.com/ weather-clouds.htm

A great source that answers questions about different kinds of clouds, where to find them, and what they look like

4 Tape the handle of the magnifying glass to the edge of page 2 of the mini-book where indicated. The magnifier will cover the cloud.

5 Cut open the slits (two thick, solid lines) on page 3. Fold the top part of the STRATUS pull piece along the dashed lines and insert it into the upper slit. Then open up the folds so the piece doesn't go through the slit when you pull the piece down.

6 Repeat with the NIMBOSTRATUS pull piece, inserting it into the lower slit. Push both pieces up so only the word PULL is visible.

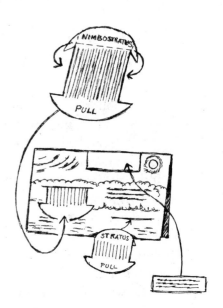

7 Tape the CIRROSTRATUS text box to its respective box near the top of page 3.

8 Fold pages 1–2 and 3–4 along the dashed lines so that they are back-to-back with text facing out, as shown. Stack the pages in order, then staple along the left side to form the mini-book.

Teaching With the Mini-book

Invite students to color, assemble, and read their mini-books. Then check for understanding by asking them these questions:

1 What does the magnifying glass show on page 2? (*Tiny water droplets and ice crystals that make up clouds*)

2 What type of cloud makes a ring around the sun or moon? (*Cirrostratus cloud*)

3 Invite students to pull down each tab on page 3. What do they show? (*Steady rain falls from nimbostratus clouds; drizzle from stratus clouds.*)

4 What is fog? (*A cloud that touches the ground*)

These puffy, white clouds are **cumulus** (KYOO-myuh-luhs) clouds. Like all clouds, they are made of billions of tiny water drops or ice crystals. Cumulus clouds bring fair weather.

Tape magnifying glass here.

2

Clouds

1

2

3

Clouds come in different shapes and sizes. They can be thin and curly, thick and dark, white or gray. Some clouds form very high in the sky. Others form closer to the ground. Each kind of cloud gives us a clue as to what the weather might be like.

1

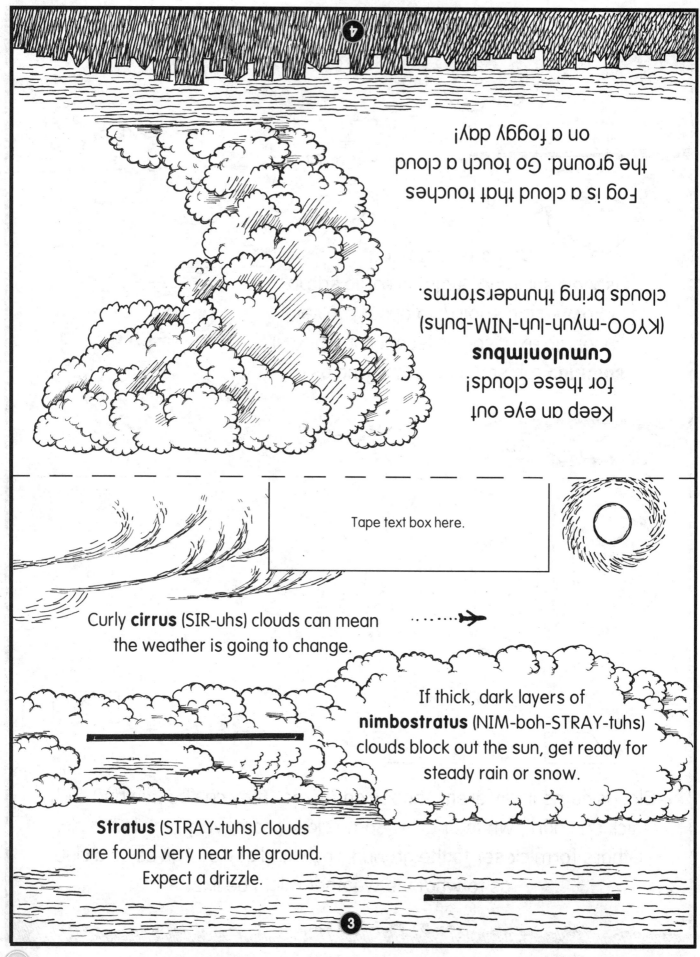

Fog is a cloud that touches the ground. Go touch a cloud on a foggy day!

Keep an eye out for these clouds! **Cumulonimbus** (KYOO-myuh-luh-NIM-buhs) clouds bring thunderstorms.

❹

Tape text box here.

Curly **cirrus** (SIR-uhs) clouds can mean the weather is going to change.

If thick, dark layers of **nimbostratus** (NIM-boh-STRAY-tuhs) clouds block out the sun, get ready for steady rain or snow.

Stratus (STRAY-tuhs) clouds are found very near the ground. Expect a drizzle.

❸

Easy Make & Learn Projects: Weather © 2011 by Donald M. Silver and Patricia J. Wynne, Scholastic Teaching Resources

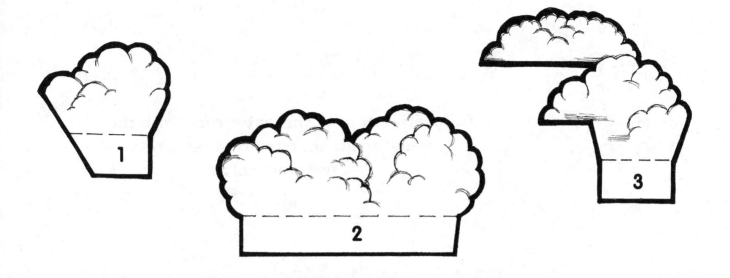

NIMBOSTRATUS

PULL

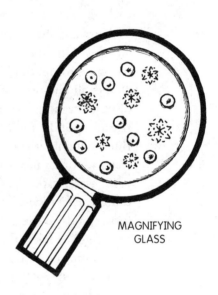

MAGNIFYING
GLASS

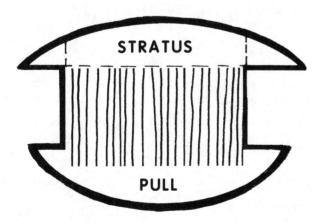

STRATUS

PULL

Cirrostratus (SIR-oh-STRAY-tuhs) clouds can make a ring around the sun or the moon.

The Water Cycle

Follow the steps of the water cycle with this fill-in-the-blanks book that features a water wheel.

Weather Center

Without water, there would be no life on Earth. Plants and animals need water to grow, survive, and reproduce. About 97 percent of Earth's water is in the oceans.

As oceans absorb energy from the sun, some of the seawater on the surface changes from liquid to gas (water vapor) and enters the air. This process of water changing from liquid into gas is called *evaporation*. When seawater evaporates, all the salt and other chemicals in it remain behind in the sea. Millions of gallons of water evaporate every day, not just from oceans but also from rivers, lakes, streams, ponds, and other bodies of water. Water vapor rises with the warm air. But the higher it goes, the cooler the air becomes. Cooler air can't hold as much water vapor, or moisture, as warm air can. At the temperature called the *dew point*, water vapor (gas) changes into tiny water droplets (liquid)—a process called *condensation*. When billions of tiny water droplets group together, they form clouds. If the air in clouds continues to cool, the tiny droplets form larger and larger droplets that eventually fall as rain. At very cold temperatures, water droplets in the air freeze and form solid ice crystals that fall as snow. Rain and snow are types of *precipitation*.

During a rainstorm, some water soaks into the soil, but most runs off the land into rivers to be carried back to the ocean. Every day, rivers return millions of gallons of water back to the ocean. All the ways in which water moves from the ocean to the air to the land and back to the ocean make up the *water cycle*. Thanks to this endless cycle, water can be used and reused by all living things without running out.

Materials

* Reproducible pages 28–30
* Scissors
* Tape
* Brad (paper fastener)
* Crayons, colored pencils, or markers (optional)

Making the Mini-book

1 Photocopy pages 28–30. Color, if desired.

2 Cut out all of the pieces along the thick, solid, outer lines. Cut open the four windows on the WEATHER page.

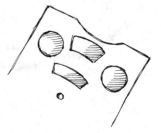

3. Fold the WATER AND page along the dashed lines so that the text faces up. Place the page on top of page 2 (water cycle diagram) and tape both pages together along the left side, as shown. Tape closed the open (right) side of WATER AND.

4. Place the WATER WHEEL circle under the WEATHER page, as shown. Push the brad through the black dots on the page and at the center of the wheel and secure at the back.

5. Place the WEATHER page, facing up, on top of the water cycle diagram along the right side. Then tape both pages together along the right side, as shown.

6. Open the WEATHER cover. On the blank side, tape the text box with steps 9 to 11 under the wheel.

Teaching With the Mini-book

Invite students to color, assemble, and read their mini-books. Have them read the FOLLOW THE NUMBERS text and use the wheel to fill in the blanks. To use the wheel, turn it so that each of the following words appears in the lower window: *freezing, melting, condensation,* and *evaporation.* Each term is explained by illustrations on the windows above it. Make sure students pay attention to the direction the arrow points. When they have finished filling in the blanks, check for understanding by asking them these questions:

1. What is water vapor and how does it form? *(Water vapor is water as gas; evaporation turns heated water into water vapor.)*

2. Where does water vapor go and what happens to it? *(Water vapor gets carried upward as warm air rises; as the air cools, water vapor changes into water droplets by the process of condensation.)*

3. What happens to tiny water droplets in the air? *(They form clouds and can fall as rain or snow.)*

4. What is the water cycle? *(The different ways water moves from the ocean to the air to the land and back to the ocean.)*

More to Do

How Humid Is It?

Explain to students that the amount of water vapor in the air is referred to as *humidity*. High humidity means there's a lot of water vapor in the air, while low humidity signals drier air. Make a class chart of the humidity every day for two or three weeks. Have students go online or look in newspapers for the local humidity. You might also want to record the temperature range and any precipitation. Ask students: Is the humidity higher or lower on warmer days? How about on cooler days?

Resources

***The Snowflake: A Water Cycle Story* by Neil Waldman (Milbrook Press, 2003)**

This charming book traces what happens to one droplet of water over an entire year, starting as a snowflake in January.

http://www.epa.gov/ ogwdw/kids/flash/flash_ watercycle.html

Enjoy a kid-friendly explanation of the water cycle with this Flash animation. Click on one of four menu items or on "auto" to set the water cycle in motion.

Water and

Water covers most of the Earth.
Water flows in oceans, lakes, rivers, and underground.
There is water frozen in glaciers.
There is water inside living things.

Follow the numbers at right and below to find out why water is an important part of the weather. Use the wheel to help you fill in the blanks.

1. Energy from the sun heats ocean water. The warmed-up water heats the air above it.

2. Some heated water turns into gas, called water vapor. This is called E _ _ _ _ _ _ _ _ _ .

3. Warm air carries water vapor upward as it rises.

4. The higher the air rises, the colder it gets. The cold causes water vapor to change into little water drops. This is called C _ _ _ _ _ _ _ _ _ _ .

5. Countless little water drops form clouds.

6. Winds blow air and clouds over land. Large water drops form as small drops knock into one another.

7. Large, heavy drops fall as rain.

8. In very cold air, water drops turn into solid ice crystals. This is called F _ _ _ _ _ _ _ _ . The crystals fall as snow.

1

Easy Make & Learn Projects: Weather © 2011 by Donald M. Silver and Patricia J. Wynne, Scholastic Teaching Resources

Weather

9. Heat from the sun turns snow into liquid water. This is called M _ _ _ _ _ _ _.

10. Rain and melted snow flow across the ground. Some water soaks into the soil. Most flows across the land into streams, rivers, and lakes.

11. Rivers carry water back to the ocean.

❸

The Water Cycle

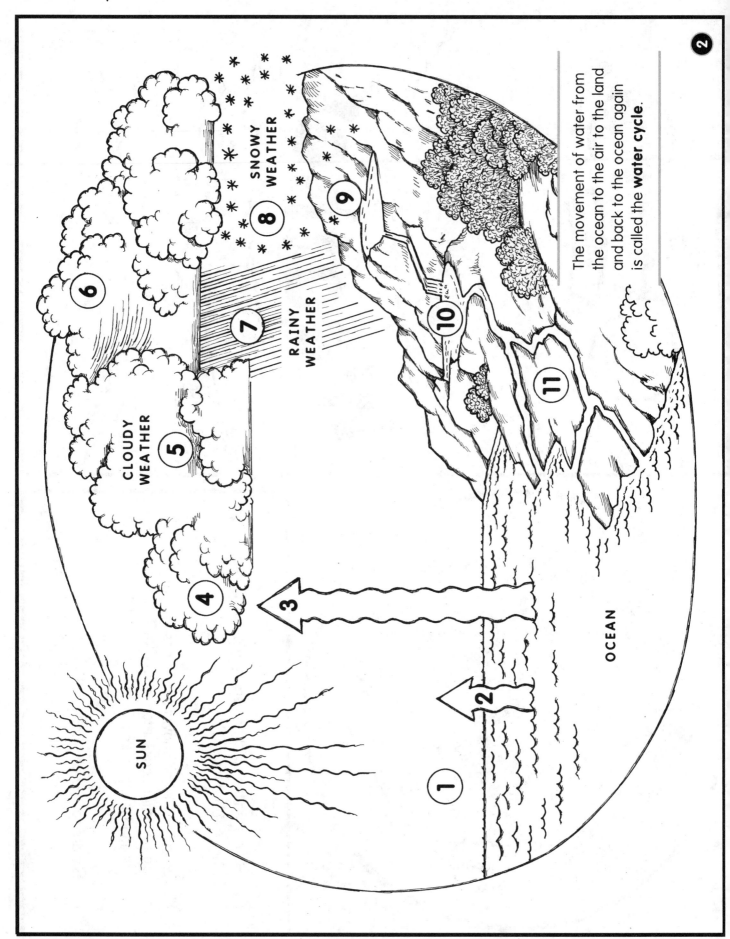

The movement of water from the ocean to the air to the land and back to the ocean again is called the **water cycle.**

OCEAN

SUN

CLOUDY WEATHER

RAINY WEATHER

SNOWY WEATHER

Easy Make & Learn Projects: Weather © 2011 by Donald M. Silver and Patricia J. Wynne, Scholastic Teaching Resources

Windy Weather

Learn about winds, from the gentlest breezes to the mighty jet stream. An interactive wheel compares the different intensities of wind.

Weather Center

Wind is moving air. Some winds are powerful, while others are gentle breezes. What causes wind? The sun's energy doesn't heat all parts of the Earth evenly. This unequal heating causes air to move as wind. For example, during the day, the sun's energy warms the land more quickly than it warms the sea. In turn, the warmed land heats the air above it more quickly. As this warm air rises, cooler air from the sea moves in to take its place. This movement of air creates local wind.

Similarly, uneven heating of different parts of the Earth, and, in turn, the atmosphere, creates global winds that blow over the surface of the Earth as *wind belts*. Some wind belts blow warm air, while other winds blow cold air. Bands of icy winds called the *jet stream* flow high above the United States and Canada. Jet-stream winds blow from west to east and do not stay in the same place all year. They separate warm air blowing up from the equator from cold air blowing down from the North Pole. Sometimes the jet stream goes farther north, sometimes farther south. When the jet stream dips south in winter, it can bring frigid temperatures as far south as Florida. The jet stream blows all around the world, not just over North America. It blows 4 to 7 miles (6 to 11 km) above the Earth's surface and can be hundreds of miles wide.

Wind rarely blows continuously all the time; usually it blows in spurts called *gusts*. The Beaufort Scale provides a way of comparing how strong winds are. The scale runs from 0 (a wind speed of less than one mile per hour) to 12 (a hurricane-force wind of 73 mph or higher). The scale identifies the effects winds of different speeds have on land or at sea (not shown on the wheel).

Making the Mini-book

1 Photocopy pages 33–35. Color, if desired.

2 Cut out all the pieces along the thick, solid lines. Cut open the two boxes on page 4 of the mini-book.

3 Fold the mini-book pages in half along the dashed line so that the text is facing out.

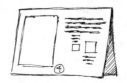

Materials

* Reproducible pages 33–35
* Scissors
* Tape
* Stapler
* 8-inch piece of yarn
* Brad (paper fastener)
* Crayons, colored pencils, or markers (optional)

More to Do

Wind Power

For thousands of years, people have been using wind power to make things move. Have students research how people use wind power today and draw pictures illustrating some of the ways.

Resources

Close to the Wind: The Beaufort Scale by Peter Malone (Putnam, 2007)

The history of the Beaufort Scale comes alive in this beautifully illustrated book. How and why Beaufort developed the scale is revealed in this historical fiction tale.

http://www. weatherwizkids.com/ weather-wind.htm

This fun site answers just about every question concerning wind: what causes it, what is the jet stream, are there global wind patterns, and so on.

4 Place the UMBRELLA piece on its respective box on page 2. Tape the UMBRELLA tab along the left side, as shown.

5 On page 3, tape one end of the yarn over the JET STREAM A box. Tape the other end over the JET STREAM B box. Then cover the ends of the yarn by taping the JET STREAM A and JET STREAM B pieces over them, as shown.

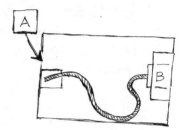

6 Push the brad through the black dot on page 4. Turn the page over and push the end of the brad through the center black dot on the cutout circle. Secure the brad in place so the wheel turns. A picture will appear in the larger cut-open box at the same time that a number appears in the smaller box. Tape the Beaufort Wind Scale table in the space next to the wheel.

7 Stack the pages of the mini-book in order and staple along the left side, as shown.

Teaching With the Mini-book

Invite students to color, assemble, and read their mini-books. Then check for understanding by asking them these questions:

1 What is wind? *(Moving air)*

2 Describe different winds. *(A gentle breeze can help cool you down; strong winds can push a sailboat along; very powerful winds can destroy homes.)*

3 What are gusts? *(Short, sudden bursts of wind)*

4 The yarn on page 3 stands for the jet stream—the band of high-speed winds that blow above the United States and Canada. Move the yarn up and down. What does it show? *(Moving the yarn shows that sometimes the jet stream moves more north, sometimes more south.)*

5 On page 4, turn the wheel to number 5. Look at the picture and the Beaufort Wind Scale table. What does 5 on the scale mean? *(The wind is blowing strongly enough to make small trees sway back and forth.)*

②

In some places, there are almost no winds.

A gust of wind can blow an umbrella inside out.

Tape umbrella tab here.

Winds blow air all around the world. On most days, winds don't blow all the time. They blow in short, sudden bursts called **gusts.**

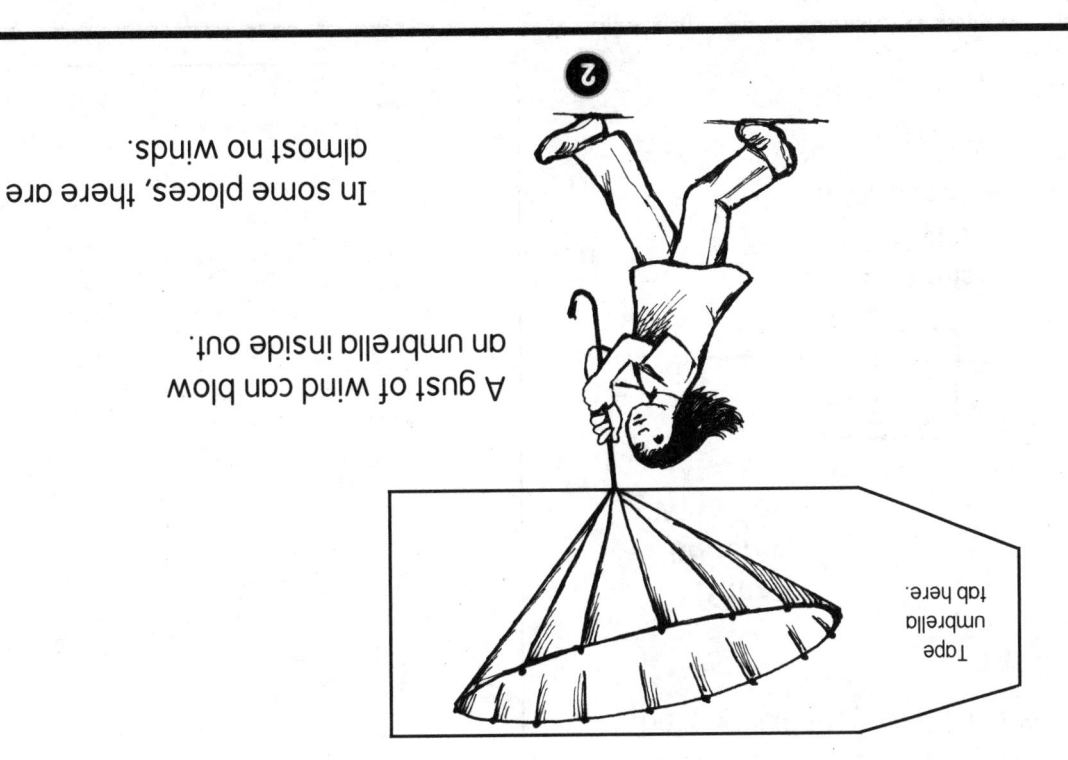

Windy Weather

Wind is moving air.

Wind can be gentle, like a breeze that cools you on a hot day.

A strong wind can turn a windmill or push a sailboat across the water.

Very powerful winds can destroy homes.

①

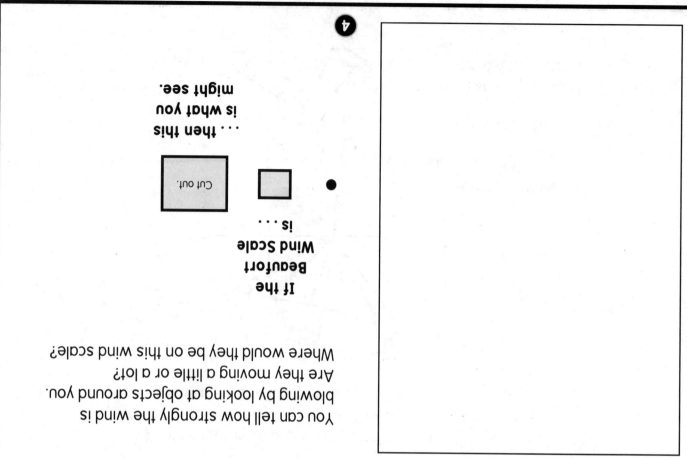

❹

If the
Beaufort
Wind Scale
is . . .

Cut out.

. . . then this
is what you
might see.

You can tell how strongly the wind is
blowing by looking at objects around you.
Are they moving a little or a lot?
Where would they be on this wind scale?

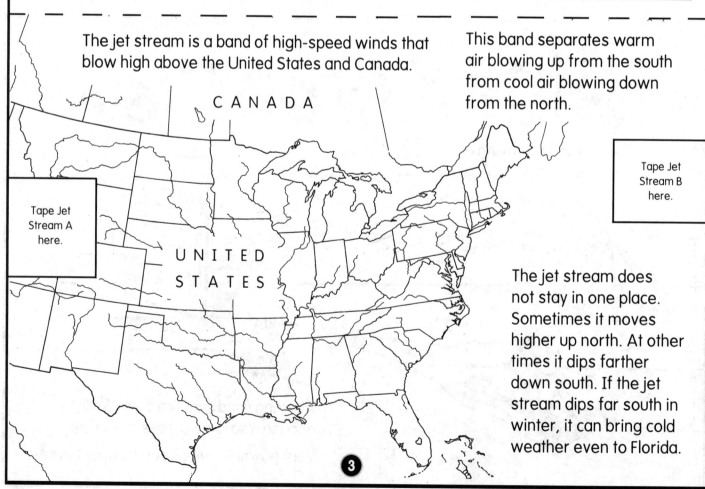

The jet stream is a band of high-speed winds that blow high above the United States and Canada.

This band separates warm air blowing up from the south from cool air blowing down from the north.

CANADA

Tape Jet Stream A here.

Tape Jet Stream B here.

UNITED STATES

The jet stream does not stay in one place. Sometimes it moves higher up north. At other times it dips farther down south. If the jet stream dips far south in winter, it can bring cold weather even to Florida.

❸

Easy Make & Learn Projects: Weather © 2011 by Donald M. Silver and Patricia J. Wynne, Scholastic Teaching Resources

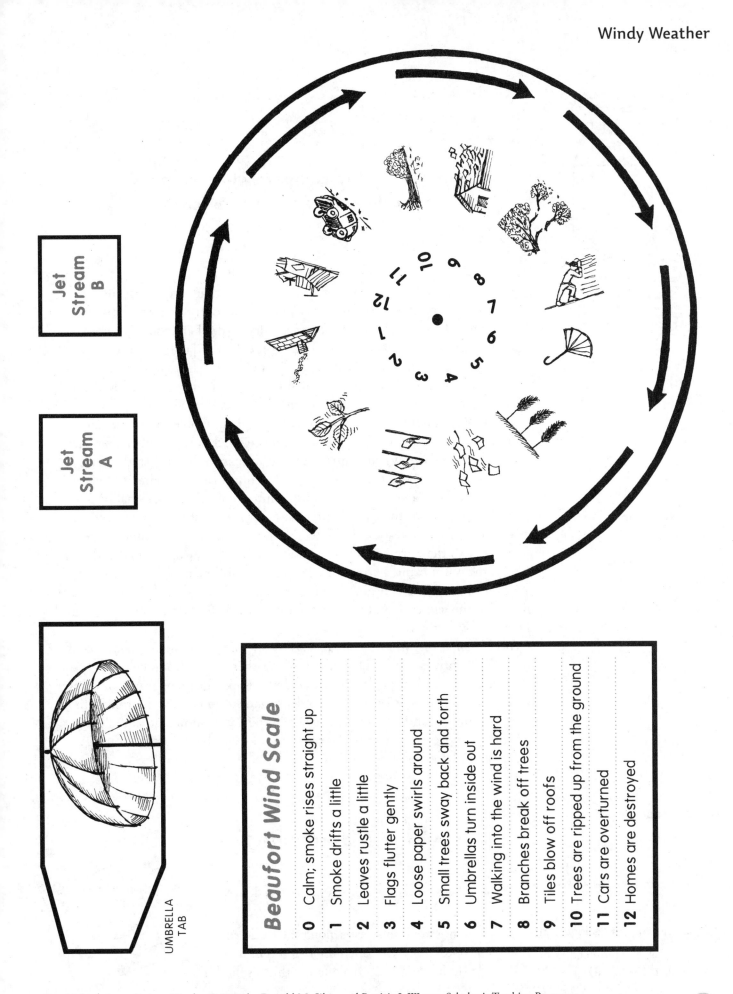

Jet Stream B

Jet Stream A

UMBRELLA TAB

Beaufort Wind Scale

0 Calm; smoke rises straight up

1 Smoke drifts a little

2 Leaves rustle a little

3 Flags flutter gently

4 Loose paper swirls around

5 Small trees sway back and forth

6 Umbrellas turn inside out

7 Walking into the wind is hard

8 Branches break off trees

9 Tiles blow off roofs

10 Trees are ripped up from the ground

11 Cars are overturned

12 Homes are destroyed

Weather Fronts

Lift the flaps to compare what happens at a cold front and a warm front.

Weather Center

An *air mass* is a large body of air that has a particular temperature and amount of moisture. An air mass might stay over one place for several days. If an air mass stays over warm, dry land, like the southwestern United States, it becomes warm and dry. Over cold, dry land, like near the North Pole, an air mass becomes cold and dry. An air mass that forms over the ocean may be warm or cool, depending on the water temperature below. Such air masses are always humid because of the water evaporating from the ocean.

Winds blow different types of air masses like giant bubbles over cities and towns across the country. Some air masses move quickly, while others may stay in one place for days. When winds push one air mass into another, the place where the air masses meet is called the *front*. Fronts bring changing weather.

At a *warm front,* a warm air mass pushes into a cold air mass, signaling a gradual change in weather. The lighter warm air rises over the heavier cold air and then cools. High feathery cirrus clouds form and can move hundreds of miles ahead of the warm air. These clouds signal that a warm front is on the way. Back at the warm front, warm air keeps pushing into the cool air. Gray storm clouds form, and it may begin to rain gently or to snow. After the warm air has moved in, the rain ends and the temperature rises. The warm air mass stays until the next front arrives.

A *cold front* forms when a cold air mass pushes into a warm air mass. A cold front usually brings sudden changes in the weather. At the front, cold, heavy air flows under lighter, warm air, quickly pushing it up. The rising warm air cools rapidly, causing the water vapor to condense and storm clouds to form. Without much warning, thunderstorms or heavy rains begin, or snow starts to fall. After the cold air moves in, strong winds blow, and the weather becomes clear, dry, and cool until the next front arrives.

Materials

* Reproducible pages 38–40
* Scissors
* Tape
* Hole puncher
* Stapler
* 2 pieces of 4-inch-long yarn
* Crayons, colored pencils, or markers (optional)

Making the Manipulative

1 Photocopy pages 38–40. Color, if desired.

2 Cut out all the pieces along the thick, solid, outer lines. Cut open the two sets of flaps (numbered 1, 2, 3) along the thick, solid lines.

3 Fold all the pieces along the dashed lines so the text and pictures are facing out. Punch out the holes on the COLD FRONT/WARM FRONT piece.

4 Place the folded piece with the three small illustrations on each side inside the cut-open flaps piece so that an illustration appears behind each flap. Staple the two sheets together on each side, as shown.

5 Look for the words COLD FRONT on the lift-the-flap piece. Tape the curved title piece above it, as shown, so the words COLD FRONT are displayed.

6 Tape the folded text box that begins, "The weather is hot and muggy…" below it, as shown.

7 Turn the piece over and tape down the other side of the title piece and text box.

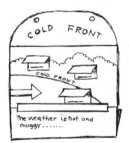

8 Insert a piece of yarn in each hole and tie it so the piece can be hung up.

Teaching With the Manipulative

Invite students to color, assemble, and read their manipulatives. Then check for understanding by asking them these questions:

1 What is a lot of cold or warm air called? *(A cold or warm air mass)*

2 What is a cold front? *(The place where a cold air mass meets a warm air mass)*

3 What happens at a cold front? *(Cold air pushes warm air up; the warm air cools down; a brief thunderstorm occurs, then the weather turns cool and dry.)*

4 What is a warm front? *(The place where a warm air mass meets a cold air mass)*

5 What happens at a warm front? *(Warm air gently rises above cold air; thick, low clouds form and steady rain falls. After the rain, the weather becomes warm and clear.)*

More to Do

Squalled

When cold air moves toward hot, humid air, it can cause a line of towering, black thunderstorm clouds to form along the cold front. This is called a *squall line*. Have students research squall lines—what they are, where in the United States they form most often, and what damage they can do.

Resources

Weather Watcher **by John Woodward (DK Children, 2006)**

This photo-filled book of weather activities describes what fronts are, then invites kids to find out how fronts form using water and food coloring.

http://www.kidsgeo.com

To learn more about fronts, click on Geography for Kids, then Atmospheric Disturbances, then the entries on air masses and fronts. (WARNING: Ads by Google appear in the middle of every page.)

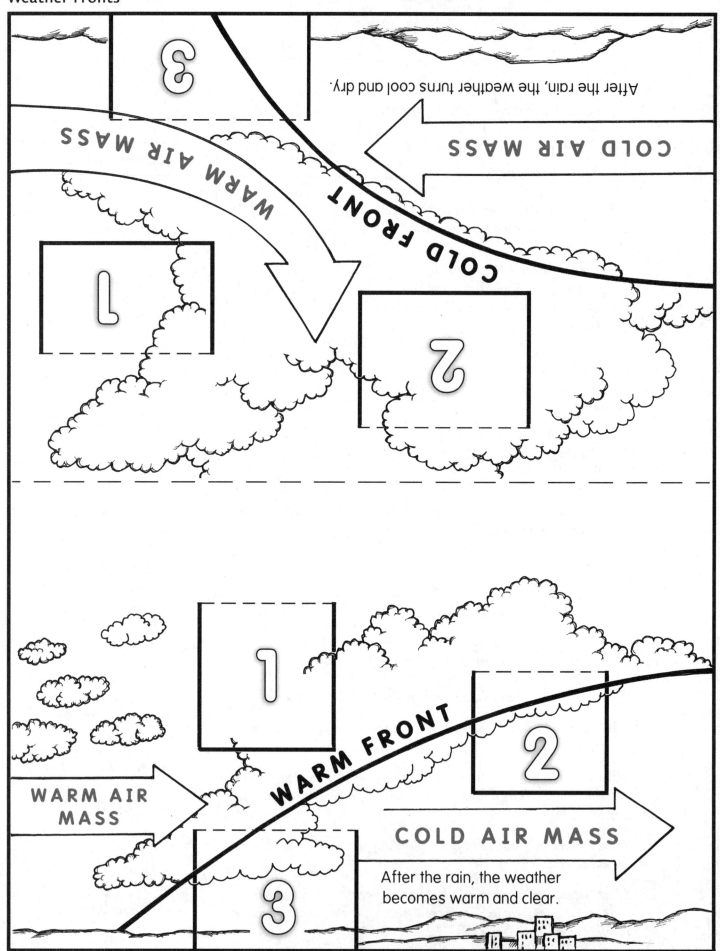

COLD AIR MASS

After the rain, the weather turns cool and dry.

COLD FRONT

WARM AIR MASS

3

1

2

WARM FRONT

WARM AIR MASS

COLD AIR MASS

After the rain, the weather becomes warm and clear.

1

2

3

COLD FRONT

WARM FRONT

The weather is hot and muggy. Suddenly, the sky fills with dark clouds. What's happening? A lot of cold air (cold air mass) is pushing into a lot of warmer air (warm air mass). A **cold front** forms where both masses meet. At the front, the cold air quickly pushes the warm air up. The warm air cools down as it rises, and storm clouds form. Open the flaps to see what happens next.

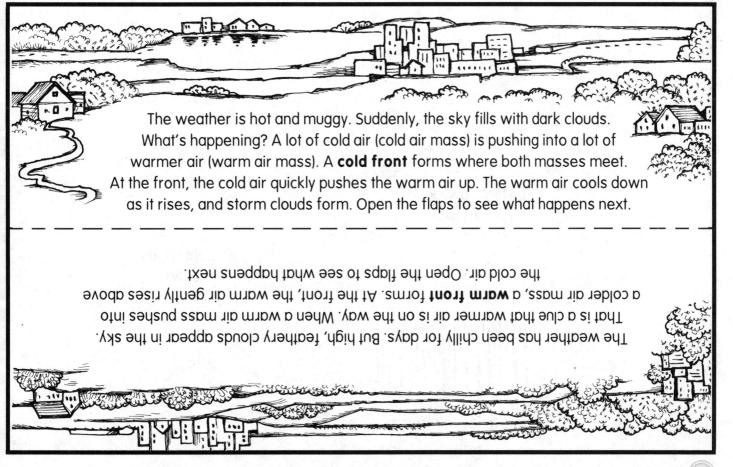

The weather has been chilly for days. But high, feathery clouds appear in the sky. That is a clue that warmer air is on the way. When a warm air mass pushes into a colder air mass, a **warm front** forms. At the front, the warm air gently rises above the cold air. Open the flaps to see what happens next.

Put this side behind the COLD FRONT.

Put this side behind the WARM FRONT.

Rain pours for a short time.

Wind blows.

Thunder and lightning fill the sky.

Thick, low clouds turn gray.

Light winds blow.

Steady rain pours.

Stormy Weather

**Follow the birth of a thunderstorm
with this lift-the-flaps mini-book.**

Weather Center

Thunderstorms are the least dangerous kind of storms. They form in cumulonimbus clouds and often bring strong winds, lightning, thunder, and heavy rain. Cumulonimbus clouds, or *thunderheads*, can pile up high in the sky.

Inside these clouds, warm air holds a large amount of water vapor. The warm air rises very quickly, then cools rapidly and forms raindrops. The cooled air then sinks quickly, creating strong gusts of wind. As this process repeats, more and more raindrops form within the cloud. The raindrops grow larger and larger and eventually fall as heavy rain.

In addition to rain, electrical charges build up inside thunderheads. These charges keep building until the cloud can no longer hold them. Then suddenly, a huge electrical charge is released as a bolt of lightning. Lightning can jump from the cloud to the ground or from cloud to cloud. When a lightning bolt travels, it superheats the air around it. The superheated air expands so quickly that it produces the loud sound of thunder. Because light travels so much faster than sound, people usually see lightning before they hear thunder. It takes about 5 seconds for sound to travel one mile (3 sec for 1 km), so counting the seconds between lightning and thunder is a fair measure of how close a thunderstorm is.

Solid chunks of ice, called *hailstones*, may also form in some thunderclouds. Most hailstones are small and round, but some grow to be the size of golf balls and even baseballs. Hail can destroy crops, damage cars, and break windows. Most thunderstorms last less than one hour.

Making the Mini-book

1. Photocopy pages 43–45. Color, if desired.

2. Cut out all the pieces along the thick, solid lines. Be sure to cut the thick, solid lines on pages 2 and 3 of the mini-book.

3. Tape the piece labeled "2" to the box on page 2, as indicated.

Materials

* Reproducible pages 43–45
* Scissors
* Tape
* Brad (paper fastener)
* Crayons, colored pencils, or markers (optional)

More to Do

Thunderstorm in the Making

As soon as you see lightning or hear thunder, stop the class and put students to work timing. Have them record the number of seconds that pass from the time they see lightning until the time they hear thunder. How does that time span change as the storm gets nearer? How long does it take for the wind to start blowing? for the sky to darken? for the rain to fall? How long does it rain? How quickly is the storm over? Encourage students to make a poster that shows what happens during a thunderstorm.

Resources

Thunderstorms
by Chana Stiefel
(Children's Press, 2009)

Starting with how thunderstorms form, this well-written, comprehensive book uses photographs, drawings, timelines, and maps to unlock the secrets of these storms.

http://eo.ucar.edu/webweather/thunderhome.html

Click on the links "How in the World Do Thunderstorms Form?" and "How in the World Is Lightning Formed?" for more information.

4 Place the circle under the cutout section of page 2, as shown. Make sure the black dots line up. Push the brad through both dots and secure at the back.

5 Take the arrow labeled "3" and lightly fold along the dashed lines. Insert the rounded part of the arrow into the slit until only the arrow tip shows. Unfold the rounded end so the arrow doesn't come all the way out when pulled.

6 Tape pieces 4 and 5 on their respective spots on page 3.

7 Fold pages 1–2 along the dashed lines so that the text is facing out. Tape the open side closed. Repeat with pages 3–4.

8 Stack the pages in order and tape them together along the left side, as shown.

Teaching With the Mini-book

Invite students to color, assemble, and read their mini-books. Then check for understanding by asking them these questions:

1 How can you tell a thunderstorm is on the way? (*The sky turns dark, lightning flashes, and strong winds blow.*)

2 What happens to warm air before a thunderstorm? (*It rises quickly, cools, then sinks again.*)

3 What is lightning? (*A powerful charge of electricity*)

4 What is thunder? (*The loud sound made by air expanding quickly after being heated by lightning*)

5 What are hailstones? (*Chunks of ice that form in some thunderclouds*)

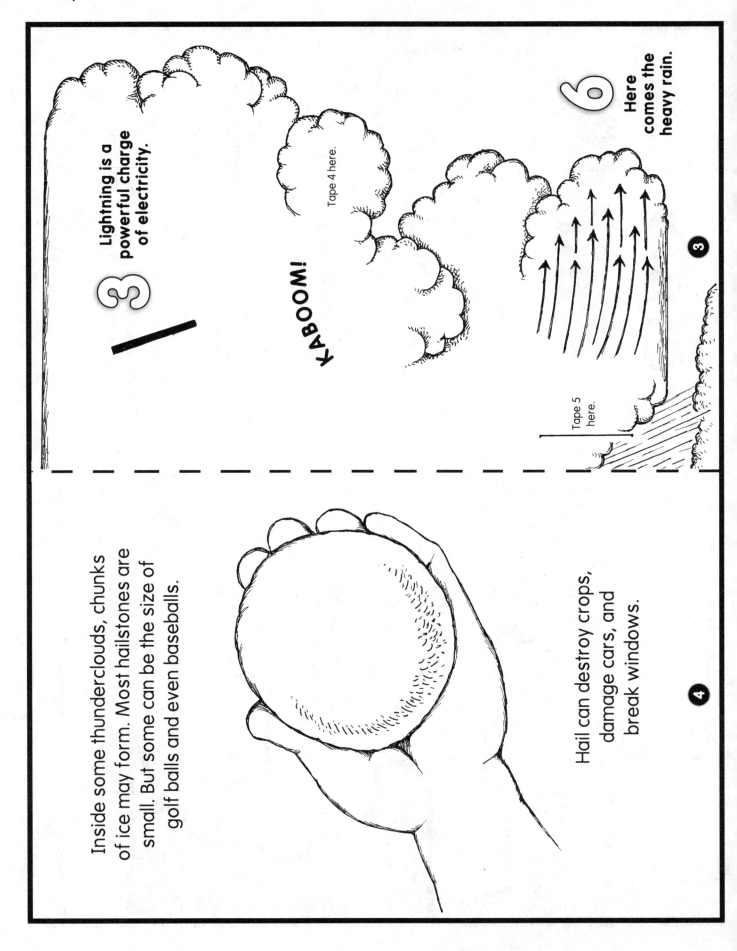

3

Lightning is a powerful charge of electricity.

KABOOM!

Tape 4 here.

6

Here comes the heavy rain.

Tape 5 here.

3

Inside some thunderclouds, chunks of ice may form. Most hailstones are small. But some can be the size of golf balls and even baseballs.

Hail can destroy crops, damage cars, and break windows.

4

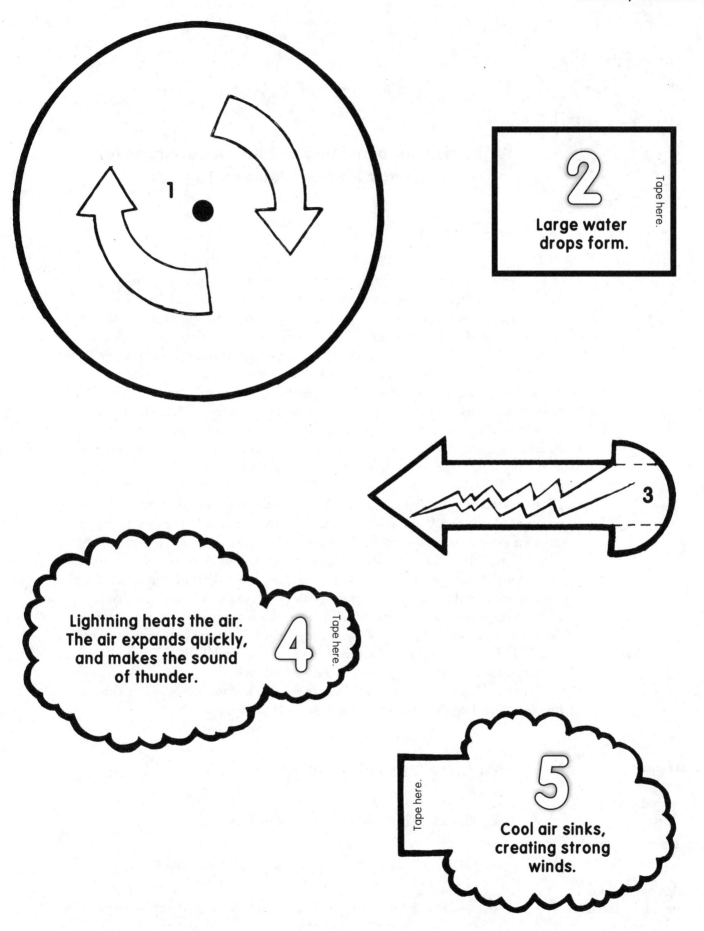

1

2

Large water drops form.

Tape here.

3

Lightning heats the air. The air expands quickly, and makes the sound of thunder.

4

Tape here.

5

Tape here.

Cool air sinks, creating strong winds.

Hurricane

With this mini-book, find out how a hurricane forms and what kinds of damage it can do.

Weather Center

A hurricane is a huge, swirling storm that develops from several thunderstorms joining together. These storms form from warm, humid air that rises rapidly over warm tropical ocean waters, usually during summer or early autumn. As warm, humid air rises, the air pressure drops and winds are generated. When winds reach 39 to 73 miles per hour (63 to 119 kph), a tropical storm is born. As the storm moves over warm waters, the wind pulls up more water vapor from the ocean. The storm increases in size, and when winds reach speeds of 74 mph (120 kph), it officially becomes a hurricane. By the time some hurricanes reach land, they measure more than 400 miles (640 km) in diameter. At the center of a hurricane is the *eye*, an area of calm about 9 to 31 miles (15 to 50 km) in diameter, where the sun may be shining. The wall surrounding the eye, however, has the most intense winds and heaviest rainfall.

Of the dozens or so tropical storms that develop every year over warm Atlantic waters north of the equator, fewer than ten usually turn into hurricanes. Of these, only one or two may reach land. A hurricane that makes landfall can bring strong winds, heavy rains, and storm surges that can destroy homes, trees, beaches, and boats; knock down power lines; and cause extensive flooding and sometimes deaths. A hurricane may die out as it moves inland, away from the warm waters that fuel it. Although it may lose power over the islands, when a hurricane moves across the warm waters of the Gulf of Mexico, it can refuel and grow into an even more powerful, dangerous storm. A hurricane can last for several days.

Using special weather planes that fly into a hurricane, plus radar and satellite data, the National Weather Service can predict the path a hurricane might take and alert people to board up their homes and move inland to safety.

Materials

* Reproducible pages 48–50
* Scissors
* Tape
* Crayons, colored pencils, or markers (optional)

Making the Mini-book

1 Photocopy pages 48–50. Color, if desired.

2 Cut out all of the pieces along the thick, solid, outer lines.

3 Fold the HURRICANE piece in half along the dashed lines so the text faces out. Tape the open side closed.

4 Repeat with pages 3 and 4.

5 Place the LIFT piece on top of page 3. Fold down the flap along the dashed lines and tape to the top of page 3, as shown.

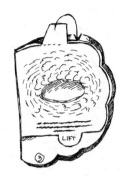

6 Tape the HURRICANE HUNTER piece above the eye on the LIFT piece.

7 Turn over the CATEGORY 1 piece. On the blank side, tape the illustration of the hurricane warning flags and the accompanying text, as shown.

8 Stack the mini-book pages in order and tape together along the left side. Open the mini-book and tape the CATEGORY 1 piece between pages 2 and 3, as shown.

Teaching With the Mini-book

Invite students to color, assemble, and read their mini-books. Then check for understanding by asking them these questions:

1 What is a hurricane? (*A dangerous storm that forms over warm ocean waters*)

2 How do hurricanes develop? (*Thunderstorms join together to form a huge, spinning storm.*)

3 Describe the eye of a hurricane. (*The eye is the calm center where the sun may be shining and the sky may be clear.*)

4 What happens when a hurricane hits land? (*It can destroy buildings, trees, and beaches; cause flooding; and knock down power lines.*)

5 How fast are winds in a category 3 hurricane? (*111 to 130 miles per hour*)

More to Do

Hurricane Who?

The National Weather Service refers to hurricanes using women's and men's names. Hurricanes Katrina, Andrew, Gilbert, Hugo, Camille, Donna, and Hazel all destroyed lives and property. Divide the class into small groups and assign each group one of these hurricanes to research. Have them report on when their hurricane developed, where it hit, how powerful it was, what kind of damage it caused, and so on. (Alternatively, if your state has been hit recently by a hurricane, have students report on that particular storm.) Display student reports so the class can compare these infamous hurricanes.

Resources

Two Bobbies: A True Story of Hurricane Katrina, Friendship, and Survival by Kirby Larson and Mary Nethery (Walker, 2008)

Amid the destruction rained upon New Orleans by Hurricane Katrina, a cat and a dog help each survive until they are rescued.

http://www.fema.gov/kids/hurr.htm

Written especially for kids, this Web site includes loads of information, from how to track a hurricane to why we can't stop hurricanes.

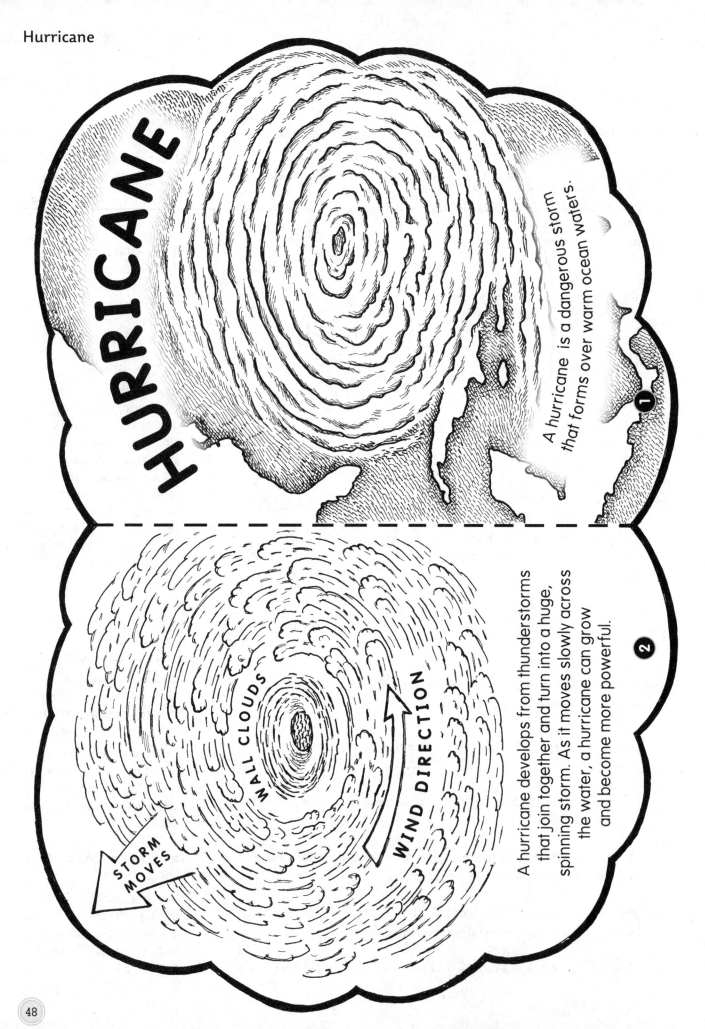

HURRICANE

A hurricane is a dangerous storm that forms over warm ocean waters.

❶

WALL CLOUDS

STORM MOVES

WIND DIRECTION

A hurricane develops from thunderstorms that join together and turn into a huge, spinning storm. As it moves slowly across the water, a hurricane can grow and become more powerful.

❷

Easy Make & Learn Projects: Weather © 2011 by Donald M. Silver and Patricia J. Wynne, Scholastic Teaching Resources

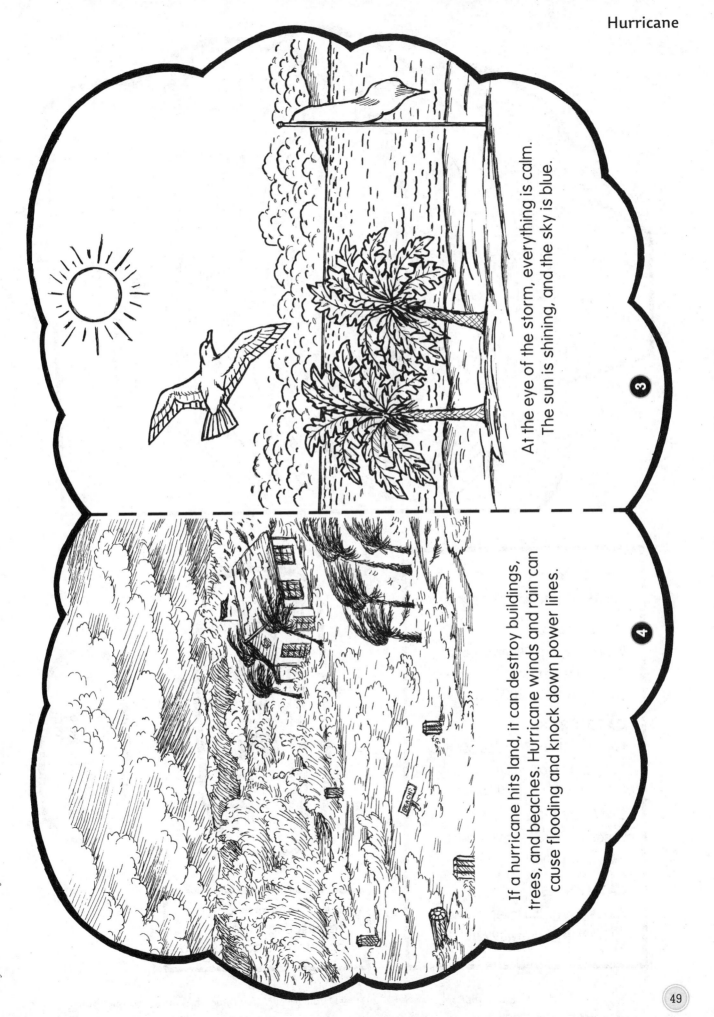

At the eye of the storm, everything is calm. The sun is shining, and the sky is blue.

3

If a hurricane hits land, it can destroy buildings, trees, and beaches. Hurricane winds and rain can cause flooding and knock down power lines.

4

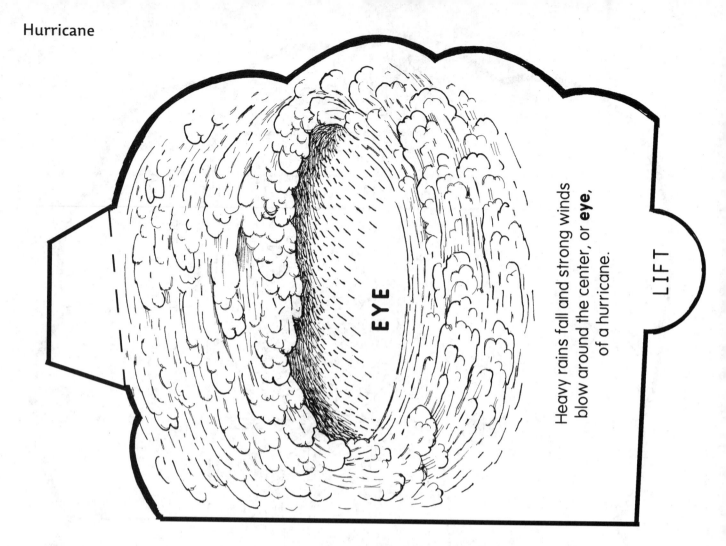

Heavy rains fall and strong winds blow around the center, or **eye**, of a hurricane.

EYE

LIFT

CATEGORY 1:
Winds of 74 to 95 miles per hour

CATEGORY 2:
Winds of 96 to 110 miles per hour
(Hurricane Frances, 2004; Hurricane Dolly, 2008)

CATEGORY 3:
Winds of 111 to 130 miles per hour
(Hurricane Ivan, 2004; Hurricane Katrina, 2005)

CATEGORY 4:
Winds of 131 to 155 miles per hour
(Hurricane Charley, 2004)

CATEGORY 5:
Winds above 155 miles per hour
(Hurricane Andrew, 1992)

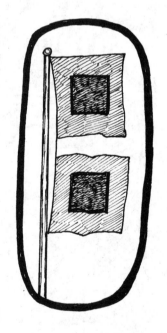

A hurricane hunter airplane flies into the eye of the storm.

Hurricane warning flags are raised to warn people that a storm is approaching.

Tornado

**Create a tornado spiral mobile
to see what gets caught up in a twister.**

Weather Center

A tornado, also known as a twister, is the most violent of all storms. It usually forms in spring and summer in areas where there is a layer of warm, humid air close to the ground and cool, dry air above it. For example, if a cold front (page 36) moves in very quickly, warm, humid air is forced to rise rapidly and a whirling, funnel-shaped column of air forms. A tornado also forms when winds at different heights in the atmosphere move at different speeds and/or directions. This difference in speed and/or direction creates a *wind shear*, causing the rising warm, moist air to spin horizontally. As more warm air rises, it pushes the horizontal tube of swirling wind so that it tilts vertically, hanging on end from a thundercloud. If a tornado forms over the ocean or a lake, it can lift water into the air, forming a *waterspout*. When a tornado touches the ground, it can cause great destruction of life and property.

On the Fujita scale, the weakest tornadoes that damage trees are rated F0, while the strongest F5 tornadoes can rip apart buildings. Tornado winds spinning at speeds greater than 300 mph (500 kph) can lift houses, cars, trees, and animals off the ground and carry them for hundreds of feet. Even buildings designed to withstand the force often lose roof parts and windows. A tornado can destroy everything in its path within a few seconds. Sometimes a tornado's path of destruction reaches a mile or two wide and almost 50 miles long. Less than one percent of the 800 or so tornadoes that form in the United States each year are rated F5. Although tornadoes can form just about anywhere if conditions are right, states in "Tornado Alley" (see More to Do, page 52) often suffer the majority of tornadoes. It is difficult to predict when and where a tornado will form. For tornado safety measures, see page 71.

Making the Manipulative

1 Photocopy pages 53–55. Color, if desired.

2 Cut out all the pieces along the thick, solid lines. Cut open the spiral inside the large circle, starting at the outermost dot and continuing to the innermost dot, as shown. Punch out the two holes at the ends of the circle.

Materials

* Reproducible pages 53–55
* Scissors
* Tape
* Hole puncher
* 2 pieces of string, 2" to 4" long
* Crayons, colored pencils, or markers (optional)

More to Do

Tornado Alley

Tornadoes are most frequent in parts of the United States known as "Tornado Alley." Bring in a copy of *The Wizard of Oz* and read aloud the description of the storm that lifts Dorothy's house. It is referred to as a *cyclone*, which is another name for a tornado. (Note: To meteorologists, a cyclone is an area of low pressure.) Point out that Dorothy and her family live in Kansas, which is in "Tornado Alley." Invite students to research what other states are considered part of "Tornado Alley" and draw of map of them.

Resources

Tornadoes!
by Gail Gibbons
(Holiday House, 2010)

Detailed illustrations accompany easy-to-read text that explains how tornadoes form, how they are classified, and what to do if a tornado forms nearby.

http://eo.ucar.edu/webweather/tornado2.html

Step-by-step illustrations and text explain how tornadoes form. Click on the "Science Activities" links for quick and easy activities.

3 Punch out the four holes on the tabs of the text piece. Fold the text piece along the dashed line so the text faces out. Make sure the punched-out holes are lined up, as shown.

4 Attach the spiral and the text piece by slipping a string through the open circles, as shown. Knot each piece of string.

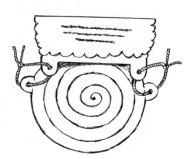

5 Tape the DUST CLOUD piece to the bottom of the spiral, as shown.

6 Tape the rest of the cutout pieces along the spiral, as shown, to indicate what objects the tornado has swept off the ground.

Teaching With the Manipulative

Invite students to color, assemble, and read their manipulatives. Then check for understanding by asking them these questions:

1 What is a tornado? (*A funnel-shaped windstorm; it is the most violent storm.*)

2 What is the tornado hanging from? (*A thundercloud*)

3 How fast can tornado winds move? (*Up to 300 miles per hour*)

4 What is a tornado like when it touches the ground? (*A giant vacuum cleaner*)

5 Why is a tornado the most violent storm? (*It can suck up cars and trees and rip apart houses.*)

A tornado is a funnel-shaped windstorm.
The storm spins faster and faster with winds up to
300 miles per hour. If a tornado touches the ground,
it can suck up cars and trees like a giant vacuum
cleaner. It can rip apart houses along its path
of destruction.

TORNADO

Look up in the sky!
What's that hanging from a thundercloud?
It's a tornado—the most violent of all storms!

Tornado

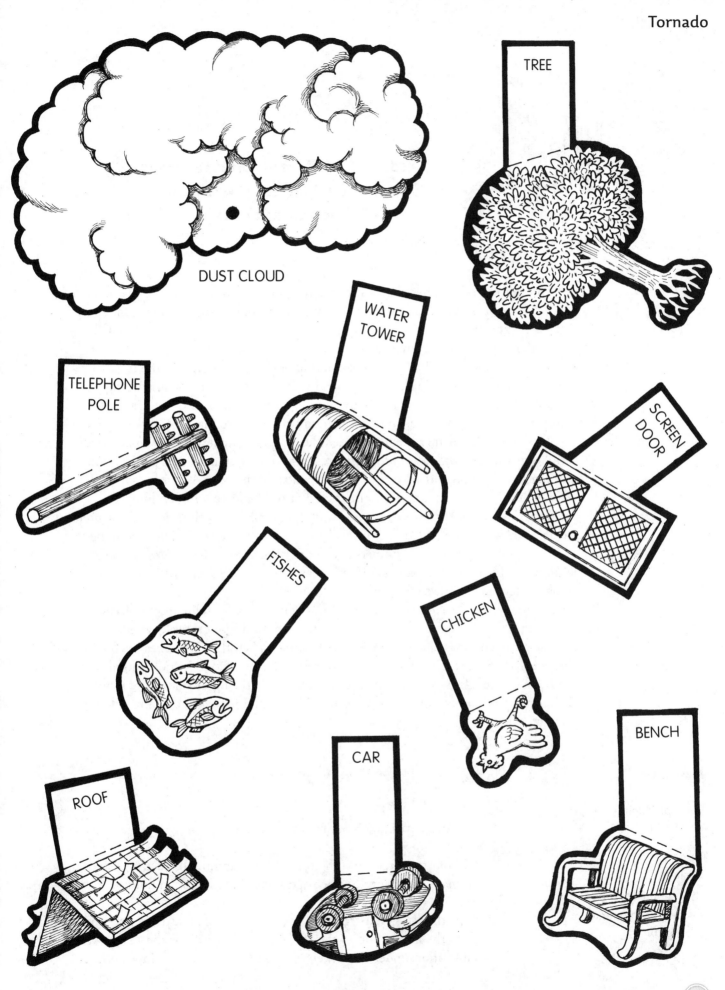

DUST CLOUD

TREE

WATER TOWER

TELEPHONE POLE

SCREEN DOOR

FISHES

CHICKEN

BENCH

ROOF

CAR

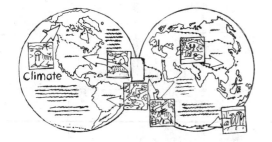

Climate

Identify different climate zones and local climates with this back-to-back map.

Weather Center

In most places, weather changes from day to day and from season to season. The *climate*, or typical weather, of your city or town, however, stays about the same year after year.

Earth has three main climate zones: *polar, tropical,* and *temperate.* The climate in the polar zones near the North and South poles is cold all year. In the tropical zone near the equator, the climate is hot all year. In between the polar and tropical zones is the temperate zone, where the climate is neither very cold nor very hot—temperature varies from season to season and from place to place.

Within the temperate zone, there are different local climates. *Desert climates* are arid, or dry. Places with a *semiarid climate* can have very cold winters and very hot summers, even though the weather stays dry most of the year. A *humid continental climate* brings winters that can be either cold or mild and very hot and humid summers. *Subtropical climates* are warm and humid all year with short, mild winters, while *marine climates* have mild winters and cool, rainy summers. The area along the Pacific Coast with hot, dry summers and short, mild winters has a *Mediterranean climate.* Large parts of Canada and Alaska have a *subarctic climate* with very cold, long winters and short, cool summers.

Natural features, such as oceans and mountains, can affect climates in places by making the air warmer, cooler, drier, or more humid. For example, winds blow humid air from the Pacific Ocean over California. When the air reaches the Sierra Nevada Mountains, it is forced to rise up the slopes. As it does, it cools, clouds form, and rain or snow falls. By the time the air sinks down the other side of the mountain, it warms up again but holds little moisture. Hardly any rain falls, creating a desert climate below.

Materials

* Reproducible pages 58–60
* Scissors
* Tape
* Crayons, colored pencils, or markers (optional)

Making the Manipulative

1 Photocopy pages 58–60. Color, if desired.

2 Cut out the circle with the title CLIMATE and the three arrows and animal illustrations on the page along the thick, solid lines.

3 Tape the POLAR illustration above the word *Climate,* then tape an arrow from the illustration to the "Polar" zone. Next, tape the TEMPERATE illustration under the sentence "It is a polar climate." Tape another

arrow from the illustration to the "Temperate" zone. Finally, tape the TROPICAL illustration to the right of the word *Tropical* so it hangs over the edge of the circle. Then tape the last arrow from the illustration to the "Tropical" zone.

4 Repeat step 2 with the other circle.

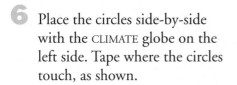

5 Tape the POLAR illustration to the bottom right of the circle so it hangs over the edge. Then tape an arrow from the illustration to the Antarctic "Polar" zone. Next, tape the TEMPERATE illustration to the left of the word *Temperate*, then tape another arrow from the illustration to the "Temperate" zone. Finally, tape the TROPICAL illustration below the word *Tropical* to the left of the circle and tape the last arrow from the illustration to the "Tropical" zone.

6 Place the circles side-by-side with the CLIMATE globe on the left side. Tape where the circles touch, as shown.

7 Turn over the circles and tape the map of the United States on the blank side, as shown.

Teaching With the Manipulative

Invite students to color, assemble, and read their manipulatives. Then check for understanding by asking them these questions:

1 What is climate? *(The average weather in a place that stays about the same from year to year)*

2 What are the three main climate zones? *(Polar, temperate, and tropical)*

3 Describe the climate in each zone. *(Polar climate is cold all year; tropical climate is hot all year; temperate climate isn't very hot or very cold all year long)*

4 Name other kinds of local climates. *(Arid, marine, semiarid, subtropical, humid continental, and Mediterranean)*

5 What is the local climate of your city or town? *(Answers will vary)*

More to Do

Climate and Life

Climate affects how people dress, the kinds of homes they live in, and the kinds of work they do. It also affects the kinds of plants that grow in different places and the animals that live there. Invite students to write a story about how the climate of your city or town affects their lives. Or, have them choose and research a different climate and write how about the people, plants, and/or animals that live there adapt to their climate.

Resources

Weather and Climate by Alvin Silverstein, Virginia B. Silverstein and Laura Silverstein Nunn (Twenty-First Century Books, 2007)

This book makes clear the difference between weather and climate, then explores how living things depend on both for their survival.

http://weathereye.kgan. com/cadet/climate/ climate.html

Click on different regions of a map of the continental United States to find out about their climate, including temperature, highs and lows, precipitation, and so on.

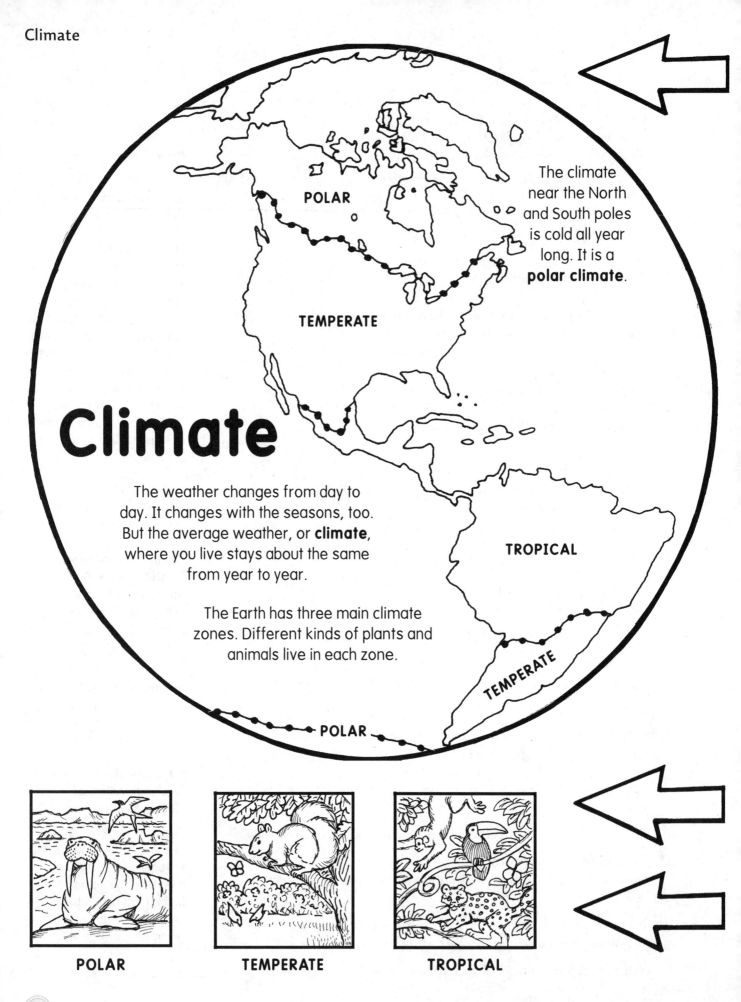

The climate near the North and South poles is cold all year long. It is a **polar climate**.

POLAR

TEMPERATE

Climate

The weather changes from day to day. It changes with the seasons, too. But the average weather, or **climate**, where you live stays about the same from year to year.

The Earth has three main climate zones. Different kinds of plants and animals live in each zone.

TROPICAL

TEMPERATE

POLAR

POLAR

TEMPERATE

TROPICAL

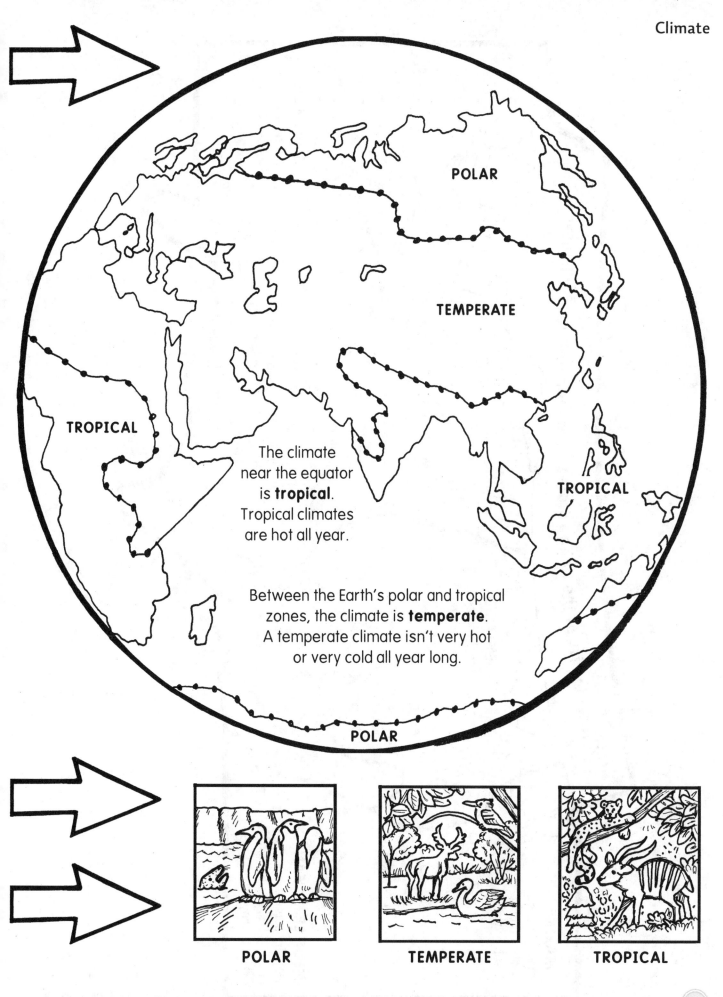

POLAR

TEMPERATE

TROPICAL

TROPICAL

The climate
near the equator
is **tropical**.
Tropical climates
are hot all year.

Between the Earth's polar and tropical
zones, the climate is **temperate**.
A temperate climate isn't very hot
or very cold all year long.

POLAR

POLAR   **TEMPERATE**   **TROPICAL**

Easy Make & Learn Projects: Weather © 2011 by Donald M. Silver and Patricia J. Wynne, Scholastic Teaching Resources

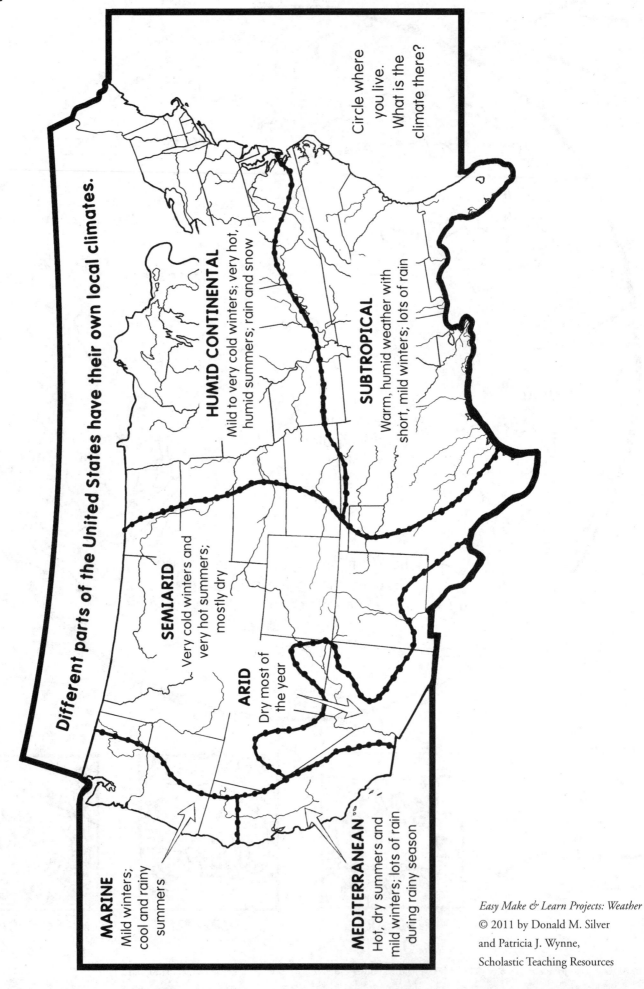

Different parts of the United States have their own local climates.

Circle where you live. What is the climate there?

HUMID CONTINENTAL
Mild to very cold winters; very hot, humid summers; rain and snow

SUBTROPICAL
Warm, humid weather with short, mild winters; lots of rain

SEMIARID
Very cold winters and very hot summers; mostly dry

ARID
Dry most of the year

MARINE
Mild winters; cool and rainy summers

MEDITERRANEAN
Hot, dry summers and mild winters; lots of rain during rainy season

Easy Make & Learn Projects: Weather
© 2011 by Donald M. Silver
and Patricia J. Wynne,
Scholastic Teaching Resources

Measuring the Weather

**Assemble a variety of weather instruments
and store them in a handy envelope.**

Weather Center

"What's the weather today?" This question seems to be on everybody's lips every day. Knowing what the weather is going to be helps people decide what to wear, what kind of activities to do, when to plant seeds, and so on. Today's technology makes weather data easily accessible to anyone every hour, every day. But some people like to measure the weather on their own, using special instruments to find out about temperature, wind, rain, and air pressure.

The instruments described in this chapter are kinds that people might have in their homes. Digital versions are also available. A *thermometer* measures air temperature. Some thermometers contain mercury, which expands when the temperature rises and contracts when the temperature falls. On the Fahrenheit temperature scale, water freezes at 32 degrees and boils at 212; on the Celsius scale, water freezes at 0 degrees and boils at 100 degrees.

A *wind* or *weather vane* indicates the direction of the wind. The arrow on the wind vane points to the direction from which the wind is blowing.

An *anemometer* has three or four small, hollow cups that measure wind speed. When the wind blows, it fills the cups and makes them spin. The stronger the wind, the faster the cups spin.

A *rain gauge* measures how much rain falls. It uses a funnel to collect rain and direct it into a narrow tube that is calibrated to read how many inches and/or centimeters of rain fell. Most people measure how much snow falls using a ruler. Ten inches of snow is equivalent to one inch of rain.

Finally, a *barometer* measures air pressure. Air presses down on land and water, on all living things, and on everything around them. The more gas molecules in the air pressing down, the higher the pressure. The fewer the gas molecules, the lower the pressure. Warmer air expands so there are fewer gas molecules in any given space. The result is lower air pressure. In cooler air, gas molecules are closer together, and so the air pressure rises. When a barometer indicates a decrease in air pressure, it often means stormy weather is on the way. Rising air pressure usually means clear weather.

Making the Manipulative

1 Photocopy pages 63–65. Color, if desired.

2 Cut out all of the pieces along the thick, solid, outer lines. Cut open the three thick, solid lines around the BAROMETER text.

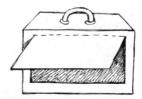

Materials

* Reproducible pages 63–65
* Scissors
* Tape
* Crayons, colored pencils, or markers (optional)

More to Do

Weather Report

Every night for a whole week, have students record various aspects of the weather from the previous day. What was the average wind speed and direction? What were the high and low temperatures? Did any rain (or snow) fall? How much? What was the barometric pressure? Make a "Measure the Weather" class chart for students to record the weather. Every morning, call on various students to write their findings on the chart. At the end of the week, ask the class: What weather patterns did you see during the week?

Resources

***Wind and Air Pressure* by Alan Rodgers and Angella Streluk (Heinemann, 2008)**

Part of the Measuring the Weather series, this book shows students how to measure weather conditions on their own.

http://www.wildwild weather.com/forecast.htm

Emphasizing that weather forecasting is an "art" that is learned through trial and error, meteorologist Dan Satterfield offers links to various sites that detail how to forecast weather.

3 Tape the back of the barometer to the front. Fold open the text along the dashed lines to see inside the barometer.

4 Cut open the slits in the center of the THERMOMETER (thick, solid lines between -40 and 80 degrees). Fold the thermometer in half along the dashed lines so the numbers face up.

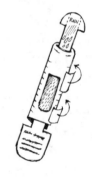

5 Fold the PULL piece along the dashed lines. Insert and wrap the folded piece around the cut-open part of the thermometer, as shown. Tape closed the open side of the thermometer, as shown, so that the PULL tab is at the upper right.

6 Cut open the center of the RAIN GAUGE and the slit near the top along the solid lines. Fold the rain gauge along the dashed line. Take the rain gauge text piece and lightly fold the rounded top along the dashed lines. Insert the top through the slit in the rain gauge and pull halfway through. Tape closed the open side of the rain gauge, as shown. Unfold the top of the inserted piece so it doesn't pull all the way out.

7 Fold the MEASURING THE WEATHER piece along the dashed line so the text is facing up. Tape closed the open sides, as shown. Place the weather instruments inside the envelope.

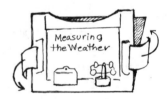

Teaching With the Manipulative

Invite students to color, assemble, and read their manipulatives. Then check for understanding by asking them these questions:

1 What does a wind vane do? (*It points to the direction from which the wind is blowing.*)

2 What is an anemometer? (*An instrument with four hollow cups that measure wind speed*)

3 What does a thermometer measure? (*How hot or cold the air is*)

4 What does a rain gauge measure? (*How much rain falls*)

5 What does falling air pressure usually mean? (*Stormy weather is on the way.*)

Measuring the Weather

Meteorologists measure the weather using special instruments. Some people use similar instruments at home, too.

Measuring the Weather

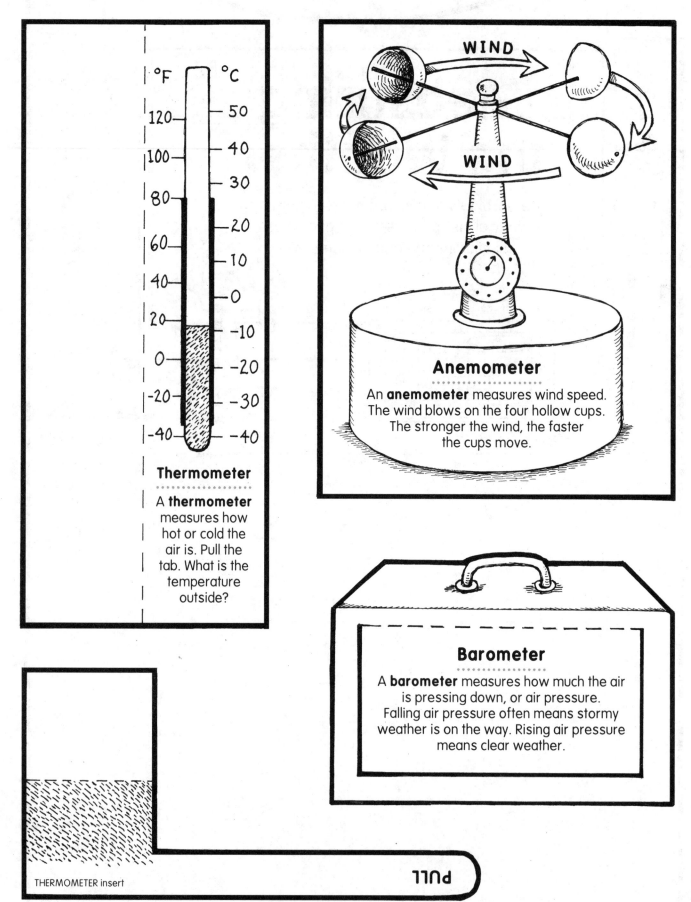

°F   °C

120 — — 50

100 — — 40

— — 30

80 — — 20

60 —

— 10

40 —

— 0

20 —

— -10

0 — — -20

-20 — — -30

-40 — — -40

Thermometer

A **thermometer** measures how hot or cold the air is. Pull the tab. What is the temperature outside?

WIND

WIND

Anemometer

An **anemometer** measures wind speed. The wind blows on the four hollow cups. The stronger the wind, the faster the cups move.

Barometer

A **barometer** measures how much the air is pressing down, or air pressure. Falling air pressure often means stormy weather is on the way. Rising air pressure means clear weather.

THERMOMETER insert

PULL

Easy Make & Learn Projects: Weather © 2011 by Donald M. Silver and Patricia J. Wynne, Scholastic Teaching Resources

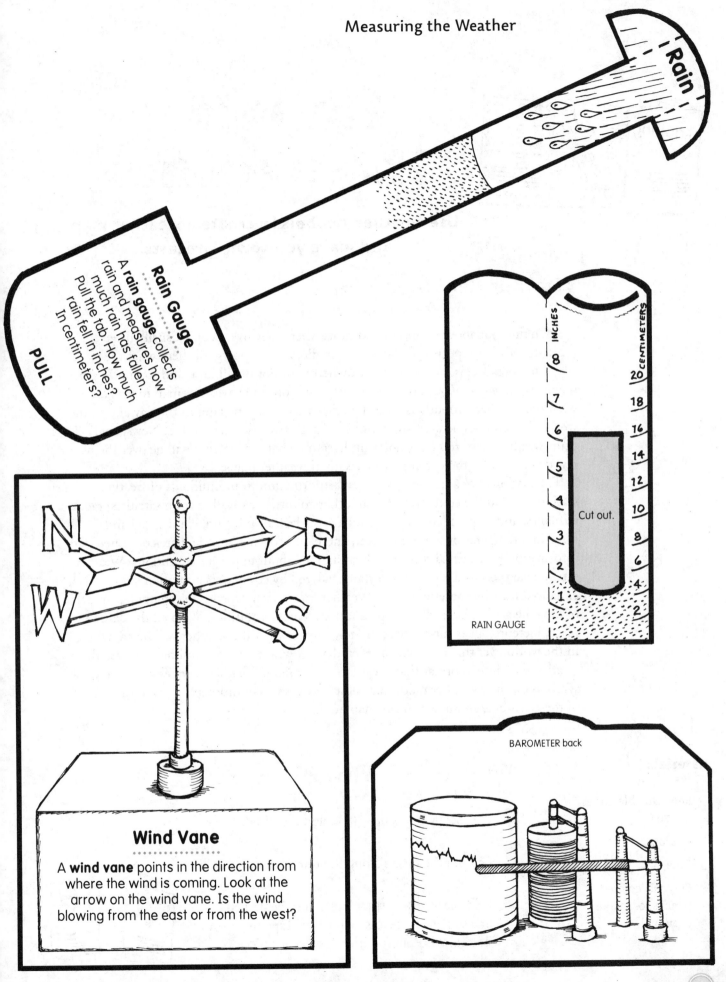

Rain

Rain Gauge

A **rain gauge** collects rain and measures how much rain has fallen. Pull the tab. How much rain fell in inches? In centimeters?

PULL

INCHES

CENTIMETERS

8
7
6
5
4
3
2
1

20
18
16
14
12
10
8
6
4
2

Cut out.

RAIN GAUGE

N
E
W
S

Wind Vane

A **wind vane** points in the direction from where the wind is coming. Look at the arrow on the wind vane. Is the wind blowing from the east or from the west?

BAROMETER back

Mapping the Weather

Use weather symbols to create a weather map and make your own forecasts.

Weather Center

To find out about weather conditions where they live, people usually listen to weather reports on television or radio. Such reports tell them what the temperature is, how windy it is, whether or not it will rain, and so on. Weather scientists, or *meteorologists,* on local weather stations use a weather map to explain what the weather currently is and to predict what it will be later in the day and in the week. Computer-generated animations bring the weather map to life. Newspapers also print weather maps to help readers understand what the weather will be over the next few days. How do meteorologists create their weather maps?

The National Weather Service collects information from hundreds of weather stations around the country and from other countries, as well as from satellites, radar, airplanes, and ships. It collects data such as surface air pressure, wind speed and direction, temperature and dew point, and cloud cover. These data are combined with information transmitted from weather balloons about upper-air conditions. Weather satellite data received night and day are analyzed by computers and often color-enhanced for easier interpretation. Weather forecasting depends on computer models of how the atmosphere will change under different conditions. With all the data in place, meteorologists can fairly accurately predict what the weather will be anywhere in the world over the next four to seven days. A weather map simplifies this wealth of weather data into a format that is easy to understand. Weather services worldwide use symbols on their weather maps that indicate weather conditions at a given time. Some of these symbols are shown in the map book.

Materials

* Reproducible pages 68–70

* Scissors

* Tape

* Crayons, colored pencils, or markers (optional)

Making the Manipulative

1 Photocopy pages 68–70. Color, if desired.

2 Cut out the pieces along the thick, solid, outer lines.

3 Fold the MAPPING THE piece along the dashed line so that the text is facing out. Tape the open side closed. Repeat with the WEATHER piece.

4 Fold the ends of the COLD FRONT and WARM FRONT pieces along the dashed lines. Tape the folded-down ends of the COLD FRONT to the ends of a blank strip, as shown. Repeat with the WARM FRONT and other blank strip.

5 Using the key for reference, cut out two rain symbols and tape one to each of the FRONT pieces, as indicated.

6 Tape page 1 to the left side of page 2, the WEATHER MAP, as shown. Tape page 3 to the right side.

7 With pages 1, 2, and 3 open, slide the COLD FRONT and WARM FRONT pieces over the map, as shown. Have the leading edge of the FRONT pieces—the rain symbols—point into the map.

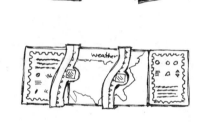

8 Have students choose five or six cutout weather symbols and tape them to the WEATHER MAP on page 2. See More to Do at right.

Teaching With the Manipulative

Invite students to color, assemble, and read their manipulatives. Then check for understanding by asking them these questions:

1 What does a meteorologist do? (*Measures the weather*)

2 What do meteorologists use to collect weather information? (*Instruments on land, in weather balloons, in airplanes, in satellites*)

3 What is a weather map used for? (*To predict, or forecast, what the weather will be later in the week*)

4 What does a weather map use to show different kinds of weather? (*Symbols*)

5 What does the symbol for rain look like? (*Several diagonal lines*)

More to Do

Reporting the Weather

After students have finished taping their weather symbols to their WEATHER MAP, invite each student to hold up his or her map and give the class a weather report based on the weather symbols. Encourage students to use the WARM FRONT and COLD FRONT pieces by saying, "A warm or cold front is moving toward [a specific state or city] from the west to the east [or from the south to the north]." Then have them slide the front piece in that direction. Have students reread their WEATHER FRONTS manipulative (pages 38–40) and report on how the weather will change once the front passes.

Resources

***The Kids' Book of Weather Forecasting* by Mark Breen and Kathleen Friestad (Ideals, 2008)**

A combination of information and activities supported by drawings and diagrams explains the science of weather forecasting.

http://www.intellicast. com/Local/Map.aspx

This fun, interactive weather map comes with layers and overlays showing precipitation, cloud cover, wind speeds, and so on.

Mapping the

Every day, **meteorologists** measure the weather around the world. They use instruments on land, in weather balloons, in airplanes, and even in satellites to collect information about the weather.

A weather map uses symbols for different kinds of weather. Here are some of these symbols:

◎ CALM

RAIN

SNOW

Light
Medium
Strong
W
I
N
D

THUNDERSTORM

HURRICANE

①

Tape rain symbol here.

COLD FRONT

This is the symbol for a cold front.

blank strip

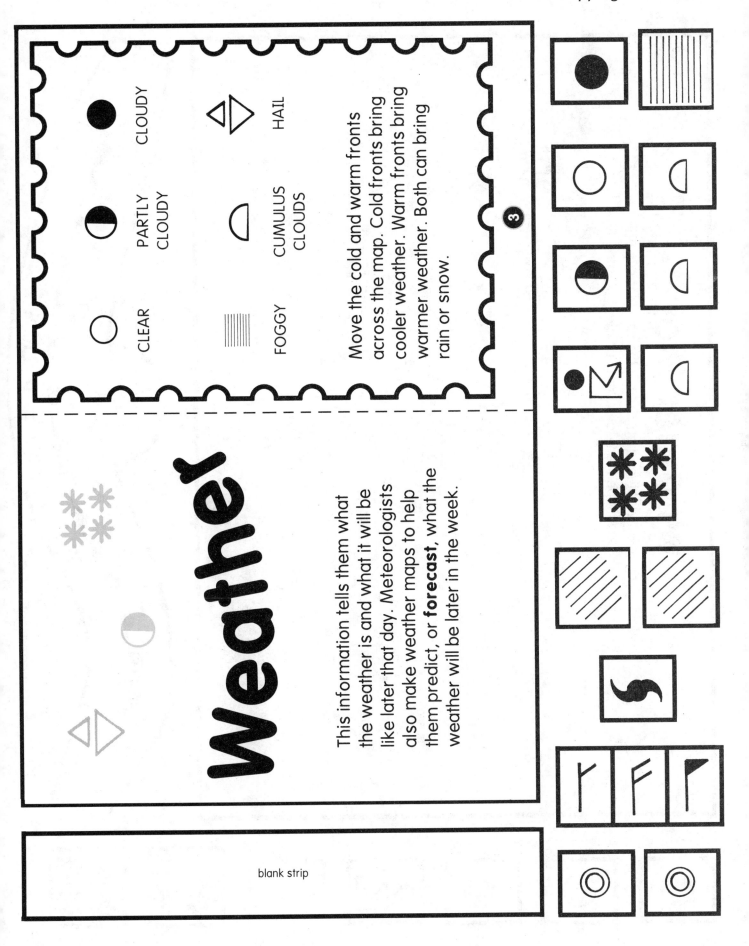

CLEAR

PARTLY
CLOUDY

CLOUDY

FOGGY

CUMULUS
CLOUDS

HAIL

Move the cold and warm fronts across the map. Cold fronts bring cooler weather. Warm fronts bring warmer weather. Both can bring rain or snow.

Weather

This information tells them what the weather is and what it will be like later that day. Meteorologists also make weather maps to help them predict, or **forecast**, what the weather will be later in the week.

blank strip

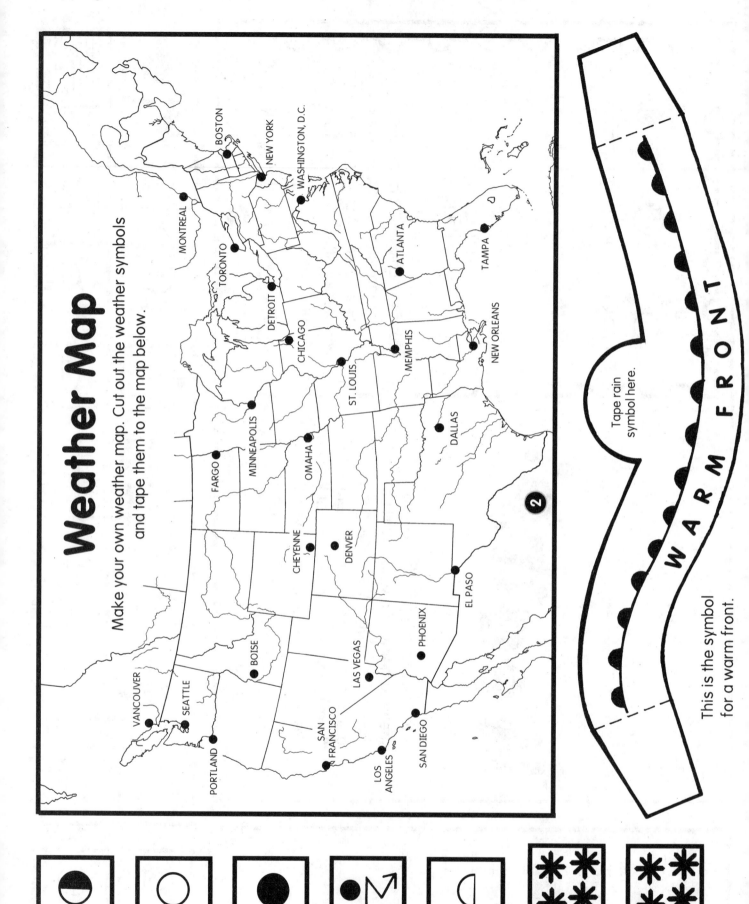

Weather Map

Make your own weather map. Cut out the weather symbols and tape them to the map below.

WARM FRONT

Tape rain symbol here.

This is the symbol for a warm front.

Weather Safety

Learn how to stay safe in any kind of weather with this weather-safety brochure.

Weather Center

Each year, many people are injured or killed due to severe weather. Many, if not most, injuries could be avoided by learning what to do and what not to do under specific weather conditions. Cell phones and/or the Internet can provide instantaneous help and information unless they are disrupted by weather conditions. Even so, there are basic guidelines that everyone should follow to maximize safety under the worst weather conditions.

Lightning kills almost a hundred people each year. A thunderstorm *watch* means there is a possibility of thunderstorms and lightning; a *warning* means the storms are in progress. Flashes of lightning and the sound of thunder are a signal to seek safety at once. The safest places are inside a building or car with the windows shut. Avoid trees and stay out of water—even puddles—because water is an excellent conductor of electricity, as are metals. Many buildings have lightning rods that attract lightning and, when struck, carry the electrical energy into the ground where it can do no harm. Even so, if lightning strikes a home, there might be a surge of electricity inside, so it is best to avoid using electrical equipment during a lightning storm. Lightning can also strike phone lines outside of homes and send a surge of electricity through a corded phone. If someone is struck by lightning, call 911 at once or send for help.

Every family that lives where hurricanes can strike needs to have a disaster plan in place. People need to know how to protect a home by boarding up windows, what to do for pets, and which routes to take during an evacuation. Never go outside during a hurricane, because strong winds can damage trees and roofs and blow debris all over. When flooding occurs, move to high ground or to the highest floor of a house or school. If caught in a place that is flooding, turn around and climb to higher ground.

Tornadoes also cause nearly a hundred deaths and 1,500 injuries a year. These violent storms can appear with little or no warning, so time is of the essence. The safest place to be during a tornado is a basement, an underground room, or a safe room without windows. Cars and mobile homes are unsafe because they can be lifted and destroyed by a tornado. If your school has a tornado disaster plan, this is a good time to review it.

Winter storms that bring heavy snow, freezing rain, ice, bitterly cold temperatures, and high winds can also be very dangerous. Stay inside and keep warm. When the storm ends, keep away from ice, especially on ponds. A person can fall through thin pond ice and drown in the frigid water below.

Materials

* Reproducible pages 73–75
* Scissors
* Tape
* Stapler
* Crayons, colored pencils, or markers (optional)

More to Do

Having a Heat Wave

Extreme heat can be as dangerous as extreme cold. Ask students if they have ever been adversely affected by heat. If so, how? Challenge them to learn more about the dangers of a heat wave and research ways to stay safe during a heat wave. Have them report their findings to the class or design a page to add to their Weather Safety Book.

Resources

Floods by Michael Woods and Mary B. Woods (Lerner Classroom, 2007).

Floods are described from every angle (causes, weather, historical) to show how dangerous they can be.

http://www.weatherwizkids.com/weather-safety.htm

Click on the various links for a comprehensive explanation of weather safety, including avalanches, heat waves, and tsunamis.

Making the Mini-book

1 Photocopy pages 73–75. Color, if desired.

2 Cut out all the pieces along the thick, solid lines.

3 Take pages 1/6 and 2/5 and place them back-to-back so the text is facing out. Tape the pages together along the sides. Fold the pages along the dashed line, with page 1 facing out.

4 Fold page 3/4 along the dashed line. Open the mini-book to the middle part (pages 2/5 facing up) and insert the folded page with the blank side facing up. Staple the pages together along the fold, as shown.

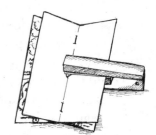

5 Tape closed pages 3/4 along the open side, as shown.

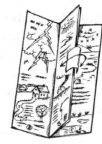

Teaching With the Mini-book

Invite students to color, assemble, and read their mini-books. Then check for understanding by asking them these questions:

1 Why is lightning dangerous? *(It can strike people and hurt them.)*

2 What should you do in a hurricane? *(Stay indoors and follow what your family or teachers tell you to do.)*

3 Where is the safest place to be during a tornado? *(In a basement, an underground room, or a safe room)*

4 What should you do if you come across floodwaters? *(Turn around and climb to higher ground.)*

5 Why should you never walk on pond ice? *(It is usually thin and can break easily.)*

Snow

Stay inside when it is snowing heavily. When the wind blows snow around, it is hard to see where you're going.

BEWARE POT HOLE

TAXI

6

My Weather Safety Book

Most of the time, the weather will not harm you. But it could, if you get caught in a dangerous storm and don't know what to do.

1

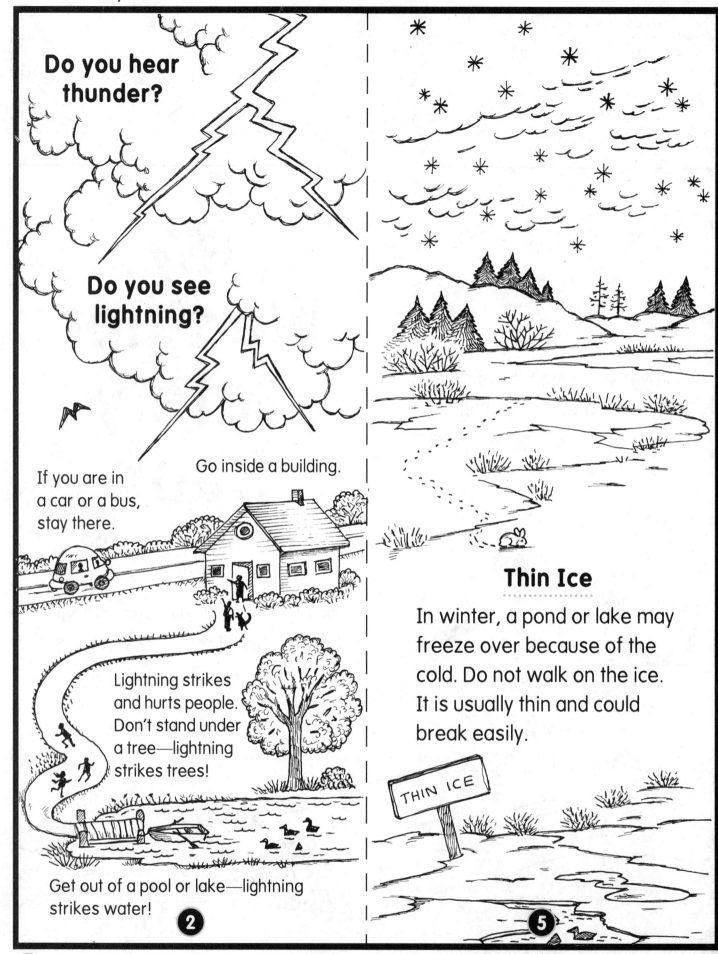

Do you hear thunder?

Do you see lightning?

Go inside a building.

If you are in a car or a bus, stay there.

Lightning strikes and hurts people. Don't stand under a tree—lightning strikes trees!

Get out of a pool or lake—lightning strikes water!

2

Thin Ice

In winter, a pond or lake may freeze over because of the cold. Do not walk on the ice. It is usually thin and could break easily.

THIN ICE

5

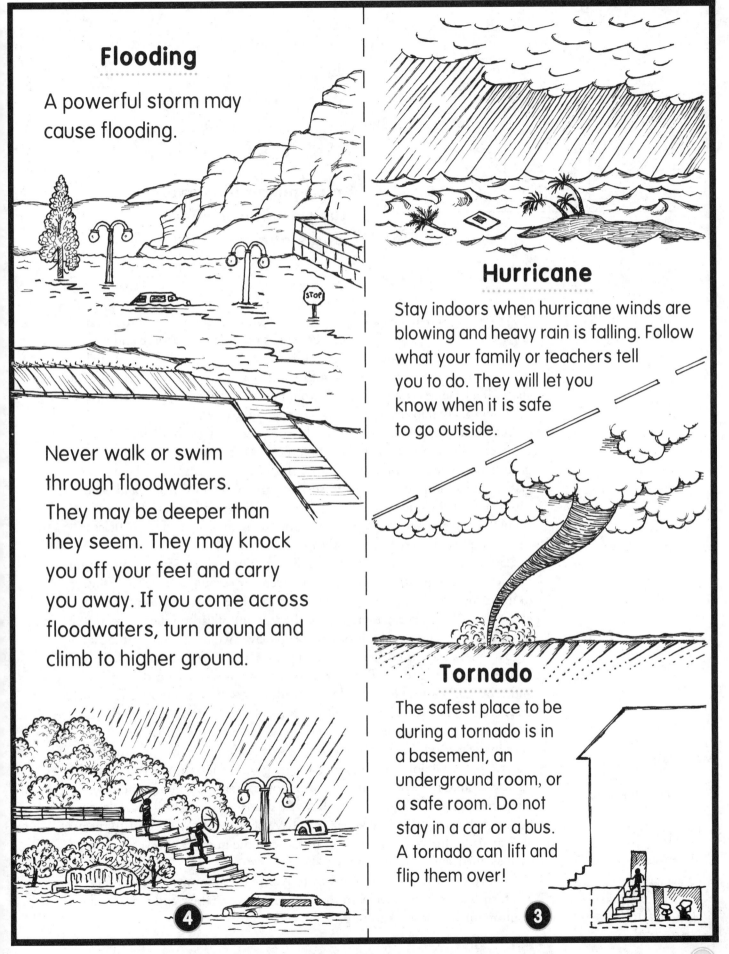

Flooding

A powerful storm may cause flooding.

Never walk or swim through floodwaters. They may be deeper than they seem. They may knock you off your feet and carry you away. If you come across floodwaters, turn around and climb to higher ground.

Hurricane

Stay indoors when hurricane winds are blowing and heavy rain is falling. Follow what your family or teachers tell you to do. They will let you know when it is safe to go outside.

Tornado

The safest place to be during a tornado is in a basement, an underground room, or a safe room. Do not stay in a car or a bus. A tornado can lift and flip them over!

4

3

Easy Make & Learn Projects: Weather © 2011 by Donald M. Silver and Patricia J. Wynne, Scholastic Teaching Resources

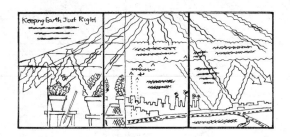

Keeping Earth Just Right

Global Warming

A mini-poster illustrates the greenhouse effect and global warming.

Weather Center

The atmosphere helps keep the Earth from getting too hot or too cold. It allows only some of the sun's energy to reach Earth's surface and warm both land and water. These, in turn, heat the air above them. At night, when there is no energy input from the sun, heat from Earth escapes back into space. If all the heat escaped, Earth would get too cold to support life. Instead, the atmosphere traps heat much like a greenhouse does.

During the day, energy rays from the sun pass through the glass of a greenhouse, warming the plants, soil, rocks, water, and air inside the greenhouse. The glass prevents most of this heat from escaping. There is no glass in the atmosphere, but gases, such as carbon dioxide, ozone, and water vapor, as well as clouds, dust, dirt, pollen particles, and even salt from sea spray, act like greenhouse glass. Heat trapping by these gases and particles in the atmosphere is called the *greenhouse effect*.

Carbon dioxide is a natural gas that living things release into the air during the process of respiration. Plants, in turn, remove carbon dioxide from the air to make food by the process of photosynthesis. These two processes balance each other. However, since the 1800s, the amount of carbon dioxide in the air has been increasing as a result of how people live. We have been burning a lot of fossil fuels, such as coal, oil, and natural gas, to power our factories, cars, homes, planes, and so on. Burning these fuels releases tons of carbon dioxide and other gases into the atmosphere. By adding to the greenhouse effect, these gases seem to be causing an overall warming of the air around the world.

As a result, parts of the Arctic polar ice cap have started melting, as have many glaciers. Such melting could cause sea levels to rise, resulting in disastrous coastal flooding. If global warming continues, the climates of many regions around the world could change. Tropical regions will become deserts; temperate regions will turn tropical. Many species of plants and animals may no longer be able to survive where they have been living. Weather patterns may also change. Already there seems to be a rise in the number of severe storms, such as hurricanes and tornadoes.

International efforts are under way to reduce the amounts of greenhouse gases, such as carbon dioxide, in the air and to reverse the trend that could result in further global warming.

Materials

❋ Reproducible pages 78–80

❋ Scissors

❋ Tape

❋ Crayons, colored pencils, or markers (optional)

Making the Mini-poster

1 Photocopy pages 78–80. Color, if desired.

2 Cut out the three pieces along the thick, solid lines.

3 Place KEEPING EARTH JUST RIGHT to the left of page 2 and tape the pages together.

4 Tape the remaining piece to the right side of the joined pieces, as shown.

Teaching With the Mini-poster

Invite students to color, assemble, and read their mini-posters. Then check for understanding by asking them these questions:

1 Why does a greenhouse need to be warm? *(To help plants grow)*

2 What traps heat inside a greenhouse? *(Glass)*

3 How is the Earth's atmosphere like a greenhouse? *(It traps heat and helps keep Earth just right for living things.)*

4 What can cause the atmosphere to trap too much heat? *(Gases and chemicals given off by factories, buildings, cars, etc.)*

5 How can you help stop global warming? *(Answers will vary.)*

More to Do

The 3 Rs

Students often wonder if there is anything they can do to reverse global warming and prevent harm to the environment in which they live. The 3 Rs—reduce, reuse, recycle—are an excellent place to start. Divide the class into three groups and assign each one an R. After each group researches what is meant by reduce, reuse, and recycle, have the groups come up with ways to implement them in their lives and explain how and why their choices will work.

Resources

This Is My Planet: The Kids' Guide to Global Warming **by Jan Thornhill (Maple Tree Press, 2007)**

A major focus of this book is climate change, its effect on life on Earth, and what people can do to become more ecologically aware.

http://www.epa.gov/ climatechange/kids/ index.html

This engaging, non-threatening, informative site explores climate, weather, the greenhouse effect, and global warming, and offers clear definitions, links, and games.

Keeping Earth Just Right

Have you ever been inside a greenhouse?
If so, you know it is warm inside
to help plants grow.

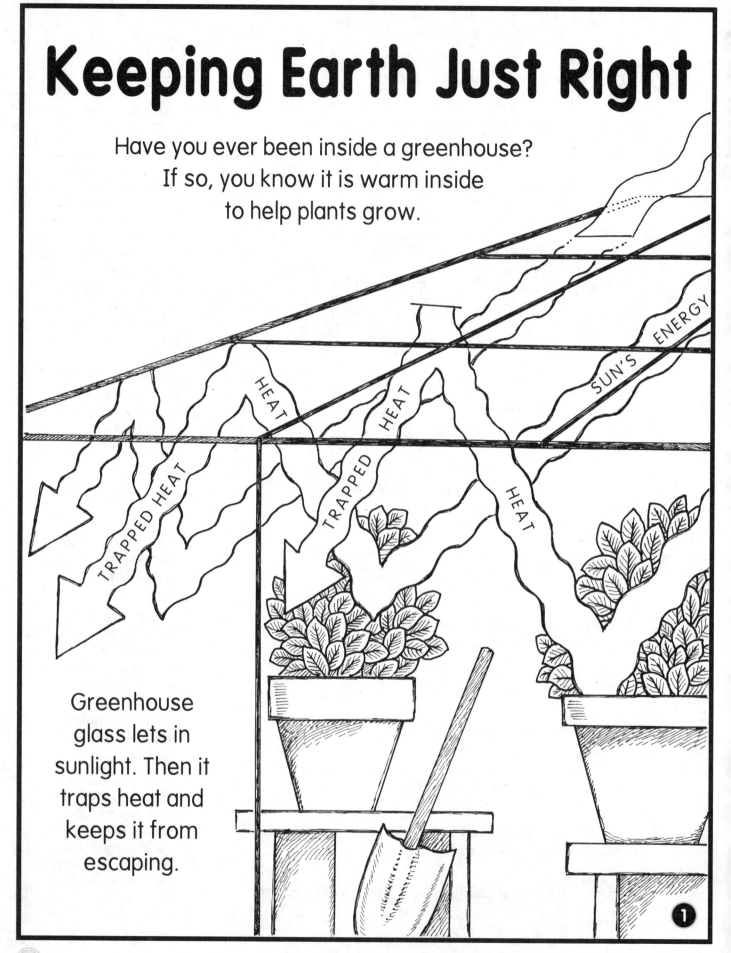

Greenhouse glass lets in sunlight. Then it traps heat and keeps it from escaping.

SUN'S ENERGY

Earth's atmosphere can also trap heat like a greenhouse. It helps keep Earth just right for living things.

GASES AND CHEMICALS

Every day, factories, buildings, cars, and other vehicles give off gases and chemicals into the air.

2

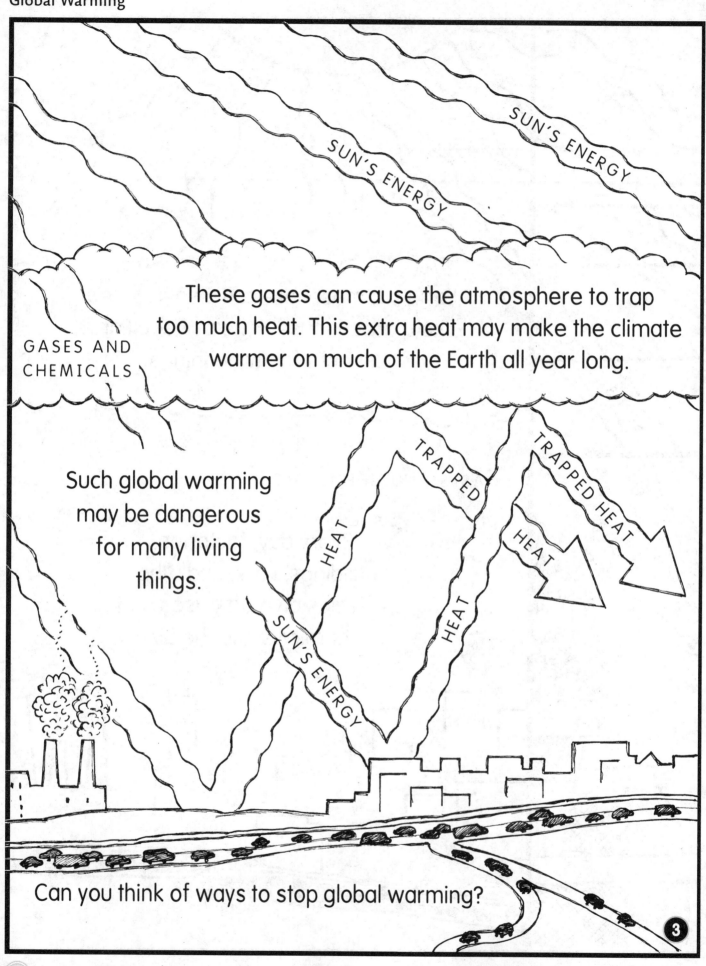

SUN'S ENERGY

SUN'S ENERGY

GASES AND CHEMICALS

These gases can cause the atmosphere to trap too much heat. This extra heat may make the climate warmer on much of the Earth all year long.

Such global warming may be dangerous for many living things.

TRAPPED HEAT

TRAPPED HEAT

HEAT

HEAT

HEAT

SUN'S ENERGY

Can you think of ways to stop global warming?

3